CREATING A SERVICE CULTURE IN HIGHER EDUCATION ADMINISTRATION

CREATING A
SERVICE CULTURE IN
HIGHER EDUCATION
ADMINISTRATION

Dr. Mario Martinez, Dr. Brandy Smith,

and Katie Humphreys

Soft Skills Pros

STERLING, VIRGINIA

Published by Stylus Publishing, LLC
22883 Quicksilver Drive
Sterling, Virginia 20166-2102

Library of Congress Cataloging-in-Publication Data

Martinez, Mario, 1967-
    Creating a service culture in higher education
administration / Mario Martinez, Dr. Brandy Smith, and
Katie Humphreys.
        p. cm
    Includes bibliographical references and index.
ISBN 978-1-62036-005-7 (pbk. : alk. paper)
ISBN 978-1-62036-004-0 (cloth : alk. paper)
ISBN 978-1-62036-006-4 (library networkable
e-edition)
ISBN 978-1-62036-007-1 (consumer e-edition)
    1. Education, Higher--United States--Administration.
2. Universities and colleges--Administration--United
States.
3. Customer services. I. Title.
LB2341.M292 2013
378.1'010973--dc23

                                        2013011213

13-digit ISBN: 978-1-62036-004-0 (cloth)
13-digit ISBN: 978-1-62036-005-7 (paperback)
13-digit ISBN: 978-1-62036-006-4 (library
networkable e-edition)
13-digit ISBN: 978-1-62036-007-1 (consumer e-edition)

Printed in the United States of America

All first editions printed on acid-free paper
that meets the American National Standards Institute
Z39-48 Standard.

Bulk Purchases

Quantity discounts are available
for use in workshops and for staff
development.
Call 1-800-232-0223

First Edition, 2013

10 9 8 7 6

To the many higher education professionals who provided the examples and scenarios found throughout the book.

Thank You.

CONTENTS

If you are reading this book, it is because you work in higher education and you care about providing great service. That is what higher education professionals strive to do. Throughout the book, we use the term *higher education professionals* to refer to student workers, classified staff, employees, supervisors, managers, and administrators who provide critical services to their campuses and communities. This inclusive definition may break from traditional notions of who is referred to as a higher education professional, but the thread that binds your interest in this book with others' is a desire and openness to learn more about customer service. That is what truly defines a higher education professional. Faculty who believe in the value of customer service and wish to improve their own service delivery may benefit from the book as well, but the primary audience each chapter speaks to is the nonfaculty higher education professional.

Until now, higher education professionals have had to rely on business books and training for professional development in the critical area of customer service. This is a major void in the literature. Service delivery is central to every higher education professional's job, both to improve service to an institution's many stakeholders and to serve each other as "internal customers." This book is the first to specifically address customer service as it pertains to higher education professionals across a wide range of administrative functions within college and university environments. The examples throughout the book are relevant to professionals working in centralized functions such as student affairs and enrollment management and to those working as advisors or in career centers. The exercises and assessments will help you implement good service practices whether you work in a community college, four-year institution, or for-profit institution.

Customer service, as it applies to colleges and universities, presents two fundamental challenges. First, individuals, departments, divisions, and entire institutions do not share a common view of what customer service is or how to achieve it. The lack of a common view is largely because customer service has not been an explicit priority on most campuses. Everyone knows that service is a part of every job on campus, yet few departments or institutions have specific service goals and objectives. It is as if we believe that good service happens automatically because everyone knows it is important. This assumption leaves good service delivery to hope and chance, and the result is often inconsistent or even poor service. It is akin to the same customer receiving two different answers from two well-intentioned staff members.

The second and more serious challenge is that people often think they are doing a good job of providing customer service, but the reality does not match their perception. As we have worked with employees inside and outside of higher education and helped them dig below the surface and look beyond their own perceptions, they are surprised to discover the many dimensions of customer service. People also experience some dismay when they realize they may be overestimating their own performance when it comes to customer service. We are all prone to this overestimation. We tend to give ourselves much credit when we are asked how well we are doing something, but then when we get down to the details, we find many surprises.

Getting to the *How* of Service Delivery

Creating a customer service culture in higher education administration is a conscious, time-consuming effort. A culture takes time to build, and tools are needed to build that culture. A customer service culture cannot appear automatically in an institution after employees attend a half-day seminar or a two-hour webinar. A commitment to action must accompany the concepts that most books, seminars, and speakers promote. Speakers can talk about customer loyalty, or the latest book on customer service can promote "having a passion" for service delivery. This is all good and necessary advice, but without the tools to help institutions and the professionals who work within them implement that advice, we are left with a temporary enthusiasm that fades after a few days.

Higher education professionals are in the business of service delivery, and they need to know *what* they should be doing but also *how* to deliver effective service. Tools, assessments, and exercises can help you get to the how, though you eventually have to put the knowledge and insights you gain from such resources into action. *Creating a Service Culture in Higher Education Administration* is built on concepts and tools that lead to action. Although "We must get to know our customers better" is sound advice, the question is, "How do we actually do that?" In this book, you will find many tools and exercises to help you with the "How do I do it?" portion of customer service. We encourage you to go through the book and complete the exercises and assessments throughout the chapters with your coworkers and fellow higher education professionals. If you are a manager, the benefit of completing the exercises and assessments with your entire team is focused discussion on service delivery and new ideas about taking it to new levels.

All of the concepts and tools in the book are the cumulative result of decades of experience, built on our work with thousands of customers in higher education, K–12, nonprofits, and private industry. We have learned from our customers, and they have learned from us. We have also woven our own experiences from these lessons into the book. Finally, experience is the great teacher, but one must also account for the work of others. Therefore, the final leg on which this book is built is the research and writings of others who have preceded us. Without these forerunners and their contributions, we would be unable to grow the discipline of customer service and formally apply its concepts to new fields such as higher education administration. In the book and throughout our training videos and seminars, we do our best to acknowledge the important work that comes before ours, even when we have tailored and customized it to higher education institutions specifically.

The combination of our own experience, the practice of our customers, and the integration of existing ideas creates a compelling and comprehensive view of customer service that is missing from the many volumes on the topic, none of which is devoted to higher education administration. In addition, customer service is an evolving field. New considerations emerge almost daily. Many observers thought technology, for example, was going to solve all of our customer service problems. Technology brings with it the chance for automation and, to some degree, individualization. Many powerful customer service advantages have come on the scene as a result of technology integration. Processes are now streamlined, and students can access registration information online, faculty can access their personnel information, and signature authority is automated for many approvals. Telecommuting is on the rise, as higher education professionals have increased flexibility to perform certain tasks and activities anywhere and anytime. From a service perspective, technology opens up tremendous possibilities but also creates some very real challenges. Few people enjoy the experience of automated phone menus, fumbling through five or six levels before there is even a chance of talking to a live person. The complexities of technological gadgets also mean that when something breaks or goes wrong, you probably cannot solve the problem without assistance. You must now rely on specialists to fix many problems, which can cause untimely and prolonged delays. Our community college and university campuses are now fully staffed with information technology experts, and we depend on them and our smartphones for just about everything we do.

Social, political, and economic trends are also changing our world—and with those come changing expectations of our customers. Baby Boomers, Generation Xers, and Millennials all interact in dynamic ways that present both opportunities and challenges. At your office, Gen Xers are mentoring Millennials, Millennials mentor the next generation, and so on. Through it all, each generation learns from the others. Diversity is happening in so many ways that it is increasingly likely that the person you work with or serve not only looks different from you but comes with an entirely different set of experiences and viewpoints.

With all the changes happening around us, absolute formulas and generic advice on customer service are no longer useful in helping you or your institution reach new levels of service delivery. You must be engaged. You must be involved in the process of learning customer service concepts and then applying them to your campus. Customers are different, and so are the people who provide the service. The mélange of personalities, needs, preferences, and interactions is incredibly complex, spurring the need for application tools that can be customized to every person giving and receiving service.

Overview of This Book

The answer to creating a customer service culture is to apply concepts and tools based on the chapters found in this book. Each chapter is filled with examples and scenarios from higher education to complement the exercises and assessments. Chapter 1 provides the start; here we define *customer service*. You will reconcile some of your own experiences with some typical notions of customer service. We offer our thoughts so that you may consider combining them with yours to create your own picture of excellent customer service. In Chapters 2 and 3, you will find exercises and assessments to help you profile your external and internal customers. You will apply new knowledge and your existing experience to customize the service you deliver to external and internal customers. Most of us automatically think of people who come to our office for help as the customer (external customers, the subject of Chapter 2), but Chapter 3 emphasizes that our work relationships are also defined by service delivery. In other words, our colleagues are actually internal customers. We then move to Chapter 4, where you will learn about a progressive concept, called the Cycles of Service, which has roots in process mapping and total quality management. The chapter offers a tool to help you analyze your own customer interactions and how you may improve them to maximize the customer's experience. Chapter 5 provides you with some information on the different types of customers you have most certainly encountered. The basis of the chapter is to help you understand how customer expectations and satisfaction work to produce different types of customers. This understanding will help you serve your customers more effectively. Chapter 6 encourages you to examine the many aspects of the service culture that exist in your department or division, while Chapter 7 explores how the dynamic between managers and staff influences service delivery. Finally, in Chapter 8, we encourage you to assess your commitment, attitude, and motivation for service action.

Creating a service culture in higher education requires a purposeful and ongoing effort. It is not a destination; it is a journey. Higher education institutions operate in a constantly changing world, so our assumptions about service delivery need constant reexamination. *Creating a Service Culture in Higher Education Administration* is a guide that will help you create a customized plan to embark on the greatest activity of all: serving others.

Mario, Brandy, and Katie
2013

I

DEFINING SERVICE EXCELLENCE

The steady flow of customer service books and webinars that offer advice on improving customer service is geared primarily toward private business, yet excellent service delivery is critical to the success of any organization—including colleges and universities. For-profit businesses invest millions of dollars in service initiatives to differentiate themselves from the competition and create what is now commonly referred to as a "customer experience." In higher education institutions, training and staff development budgets devoted to service training are difficult to justify in an environment of scarce resources or shrinking state dollars. Training investments for employees across campuses are focused disproportionately on technical training. Directors and managers can easily justify training for a newly installed software system or perhaps a half-day informational course on new federal regulations pertaining to student aid, but initiatives to improve service delivery or other soft skills–type training usually elicit administrative requests for clarification if not outright denial.

Do Customer Service Concepts Apply to Higher Education?

Part of the challenge of making service training and thus service competency an integral part of higher education institutions is the language that accompanies the topic. Institutions, public and private, two- and four-year, still struggle with terms such as *customer* and *service*, which creates a stumbling block to initiatives that can truly improve teamwork and interaction with anyone a particular office on campus happens to serve. It is understandable that many colleges and universities are hesitant to automatically adopt language they associate with for-profit businesses. Are students, parents, and faculty really customers of the registrar or financial aid office? Some campus offices prefer to call them clients, while others avoid either customer or client. For many higher education professionals, it is somewhat akin to the dilemma a department of corrections agency might have calling a prisoner a customer, or perhaps a health and human services department referring to a recipient of government assistance as a client.

Disputes aside, the foundational principles and ideas that underlie excellent service delivery are as applicable to those working in higher education as they are to someone working at a grocery store or a five-star hotel. The implementation of these foundational principles accomplishes two important goals: to improve internal teamwork and to more effectively fulfill the needs of those who come to us for service.

Private business has not cornered the market on effective service delivery. Excellent examples exist in all types of institutions and campuses, where different offices and entire divisions are fulfilling the dual goals of strengthening teamwork and service delivery to end customers. In a College of Health Sciences' (CHS) advising office with which we are familiar, advisors believe in and demonstrate the principles of good service delivery daily, with students and each other. This particular office has a baseline philosophy of no "runaround." If an advisor does not have an answer for a student or the student has a need outside of the advising office, it is not uncommon to find a CHS advisor and student walking across campus to enlist the help of another office. The advisors in this office have also been trained to follow good communication protocol with each other. While written electronic communication can be efficient, advisors thoughtfully determine when face-to-face interaction between and among team members may be preferable to an instant message or e–mail. In this office, critical issues are not discussed via e–mail. When disagreements occur, staff automatically invoke the conflict resolutions skills that are a mandatory part of training for everyone in the office. There is a premium placed on soft skills.

The example this particular advising office brings out is this: implementation of good service principles is based on awareness, philosophy (values), and application. It is often the application that we struggle with. Part of the challenge of implementing effective service principles in higher education is that many of the experts who try to build awareness of good service values do not work within higher education. They are not from higher education and do not know the context of postsecondary education or the culture of the many different offices across a campus. Existing resources, in the form of books and training curriculum on service delivery, are virtually all from people who have never worked on a college campus. Their advice remains very general and difficult to apply. Even though many of the principles of effective service are applicable across industries, implementation in different settings requires an understanding and appreciation of a particular field. Someone may offer general advice on *what* we should be doing, but without an understanding of the industry, they do not have a good sense of *how* we might do it. To maximize the *what* and the *how*, the examples and tools in this chapter—and in all of the book's chapters—draw on our own work in higher education and the experiences of higher education professionals across scores of campuses. Still, we can learn much from famous hotel chains and amusement park companies that have achieved notable service levels as they explain their processes, practices, and philosophies. It is beneficial, therefore, for us to draw on our own experiences with different types of organizations and capture effective examples of service. An essential ingredient to defining service excellence for your institution, then, is to figure out which service practices from a broad range of industries you believe might apply to higher education. After you do this, it becomes easier to customize effective service delivery practices that make sense for your office environment, wherever it resides within the higher education world.

Starting the Service Excellence Journey

The question now becomes: Where to begin? Knowing where to begin is always the difficult part, whether you're writing a memo, training for a marathon, or facing the daunting task of cleaning your house. The good news: once we get started, it is easy to get into the "flow" of things and make steady progress. We will start the process of strengthening service delivery on your campus with a couple of key points:

- We won't get caught up in the language of "customer," "client," "customer service," or any other such words. What is important are the concepts. We will tend to stay with the language of customers and service since those words still, for the most part, denote an emphasis on effective interaction with colleagues and those outside your immediate office environment who come to you for help (e.g., students, parents, and faculty).
- We will draw on your experiences, from both inside and outside of higher education, so you can create a customized view of effective service delivery that applies to and works for you.
- Building a service culture in your office and on your campus is a journey, not a destination. We will start by taking you through the steps in this process: defining effective service delivery in general.

Step 1: Identify Excellent Service Experiences

Though many of us know it when we receive it, good service is difficult to define. This is largely because good service cannot be boiled down to one word or sentence. Think about your own experiences for a moment. You may have had the pleasant and perhaps unexpected experience of receiving the VIP treatment from a clerk at the convenience store near your home as you picked up a morning treat on your way to work. Of course, all of us have had those great, memorable service experiences while on vacation, but excellent service is all around us (so is poor service, but more on that later) as we go about our daily business. As you think about the good service experiences you have had, you quickly realize that different organizations deliver different things, and the quality of service you receive may be a function of the person delivering that service and even your enthusiasm for the product or service you receive. Yet, some common characteristics define good service, no matter where you may have received that service. That is because these characteristics align with some basic laws of human interaction that create favorable impressions of service delivery in virtually all situations.

The best way to begin identifying these common characteristics is to cast a wide net. Good explanations, definitions, and actions are best achieved by going from the general to the specific, all based on your experiences. This eventually gets you to application. Thus, a good first step is to think of some organizations that you generally associate with excellent customer service. You are starting out "in general" because you are to think about good service that you, personally, have received from any type of organization other than a higher education–related institution. Higher education examples or those instances related to your particular office are more specific, and we will work toward those descriptions after we build a general description of excellent service delivery.

What are two organizations that you equate with excellent service? When asked to list excellent service organizations, people automatically list companies like Disney, the Ritz-Carlton, or Southwest Airlines. Certainly, Disney offers a magical experience that is known across the globe, and Southwest Airlines has low prices, crew members who have a great sense of humor, and point-to-point service to numerous destinations. While these are examples of excellent companies, they are not organizations from which most of us receive service on a daily, weekly, or even monthly basis. For purposes of Exercise 1, try to think of local organizations with which you have regular contact. The goal is to identify two local organizations that consistently deliver excellent service to you. You may receive regular service from an organization over the phone or via the Internet, and such organizations also qualify for purposes of the exercise. The main point is that these two organizations, whether for-profit or nonprofit, have consistently and regularly met your standard for delivering excellent service. Write the names of the two organizations that come to mind in the spaces numbered 1 and 2, in Exercise 1.

EXERCISE 1
Two Organizations That Deliver Excellent Service to You

1. _Disney_

2. _Southwest_

You may have listed a restaurant, bank branch, retail store, library, or automotive repair shop in your town. Now that you have identified these organizations, ask yourself: What is it that makes them so good at delivering excellent service? Most people, when asked to make a list like you just completed in Exercise 1, think not of some impersonal organization but of the experience of receiving the service, in concrete terms. If their interaction with the company or organization requires their physical presence to receive the service, they think about the location and the people who served them. It is also common to recall the sequence of events that defined the service they received: the conversation that took place, whether other customers were present and how that influenced your wait time, or even the look and feel of the location or office. For the organizations you listed, you may be so familiar with the company that you automatically think about a specific department or person that provides the service you seek.

Maybe the service you received was over the phone rather than in person. In this case, we generally recall specifics about the conversation that made us feel like this was a good customer experience. We may even remember some steps we had followed to get what we needed, or that we were pleasantly surprised not to have gotten confused by complex instructions because everything was so simple.

Step 2: Define Excellent Service Delivery

Whatever organizations you listed, the question now becomes: What specifically did this organization and its employees do to make you feel you received excellent service? How would you describe the service delivery you received? To truly define good service, you must think about what you personally associate with it. Relive those pleasant service experiences you received from the organizations you listed in Exercise 1. Now, in Exercise 2, list words, phrases, or adjectives that you associate with a good service experience.

EXERCISE 2
Good Customer Service (list descriptors in the space provided)

Employees have a contagious positive spirit

make customers feel special

happy place

How does your list look? We have conducted this exercise over the last ten years with higher education professionals, pilots, human resources teams, and dozens of other organizations and associations—including a team of physicists working at a university! There is certainly some degree of variability in the lists people make, but there is also a striking degree of similarity in the attributes people associate with good service delivery. Here is a top ten list of attributes we have gathered over the years from different audiences and groups:

1. Positive attitude
2. Attentive, friendly, and sincere
3. Provides answers or finds the answers, but doesn't make excuses
4. Consistent
5. Listens
6. Flexibility
7. Knowledgeable
8. Keeps the customer informed
9. Honest
10. Quick response to questions or requests

How does your list compare with ours? There is probably overlap between the two. You may have used some different wording, but many of the general ideas of excellent service delivery seem to apply to any organization—including institutions of higher education. Let's take the first attribute from our list as an example. In 90% of the workshops we have conducted, the idea of "positive attitude" emerges almost immediately. There are very few instances when we would rather deal with someone who has a negative attitude than someone with a positive attitude. Of course, there are exceptions. If you need your appendix removed, and you have the choice between a positive doctor who doesn't know what he is doing and a negative doctor who has done this a hundred times before, you are probably going to choose the negative doctor with the experience. In general, though, most of us prefer to receive service from someone who has a positive attitude. As you make your way down your own list, you will likely find that these items are assets in almost any service setting.

Assuming that your list was similar to ours, take a look at our top ten list one more time. A final question usually surfaces whenever teams develop a list to describe good customer service: How many of the ten items on the list describe *technical skills* versus what we might call *people skills* (or soft skills)? The only item that really sticks out as strictly a technical skill is Item 7, knowledgeable. This is not to underplay the importance of knowledge or any other technical skills that are involved in delivering superior service, but a quick examination of the list does make it clear that people skills are a huge part of the service equation. Many of us have even received good service from employees who didn't have a lot of background or knowledge, but these people were honest with us (Item 9) and assured us that they were going to find the answer (Item 3) and follow up. We still ended up feeling like we received good service. While we all expect those who are delivering a service to have at least a minimal level of technical skill, people skills really do matter in the service delivery equation. Good service skills and good people skills are synonymous.

Step 3: Be Conscious of Bad Service Delivery

Although most of us would prefer to look back on good memories, the reality is that we must also learn from our bad experiences. That is where Step 3 comes in. It is just as important to examine our bad service experiences as it is the good ones because we then become very conscious about the things we shouldn't be doing. We can all get better at service delivery if we remind ourselves of both sides of the service coin: things we should be doing and things we shouldn't be doing.

Another reason for explicitly describing bad experiences is that they leave an impression, thus providing a constant reminder of behaviors we should avoid. In fact, most people are better able to recall and describe bad experiences more accurately than they are good ones. Bad experiences are accompanied by intense emotions, which make them memorable. Psychologists tell us that emotional experiences leave a deep imprint in our minds, which is probably why customer service gurus often say things like, "It takes nine good experiences to make up for one bad experience." It may be the pessimistic side of us all, but it does seem as if we tend to notice the one dirty speck on the windshield and not the other 99% that is clean.

Just as you cast a wide net in Steps 1 and 2 to identify exemplary organizations and good service attributes, it is now time to relive a bad service experience. Once again, think of a personal experience you lived through. This time pick an example of what not to do when delivering service. For this exercise, you can think of a national or local organization, or one that delivered bad service one time, prompting you to vow never to use its service again. Maybe you even gave the company a second chance, only to have it drop the ball again.

Was your bad experience in a store or restaurant? Was it when you were calling a help desk and trying to get some information? Did you have to navigate through a long, automated phone system and then repeat all of your information when you finally reached a live human being? Perhaps you received a bill from the hospital that seemed incorrect, and you visited the billing department, only to leave in total frustration? Once again, as you think about this experience, stay away from higher education-related examples for now.

We won't be listing the organizations as we did in Exercise 1; rather, we will skip immediately to the process of identifying those characteristics associated with bad service. As difficult as it is, try to relive that unpleasant service experience you just thought about. What specifically made you feel like you received poor service? How would you describe the service? To define bad service, think about what you personally associate with it. In Exercise 3, list words, phrases, or adjectives you associate with bad service delivery.

EXERCISE 3
Bad Customer Service (list descriptors in the space provided)

lack of empathy

inflexibility

How did your bad service list look? Did you find yourself actually getting a bit worked up as you began reliving your bad service experience? Most people do, because the memory is often just as strong as the actual experience. In fact, we often get angrier when we relive the bad experience than when we actually experienced it. We think about things we should have said or done so the service provider would have known exactly what we were feeling. Even though bad memories evoke bad feelings, the purpose of Exercise 3 is to learn from these bad experiences.

So, to move forward, let's compare your list with ours. Just as we gathered a list of good service attributes, we have also saved our feedback from hundreds of training sessions where the group task was to describe bad service. Here is a top ten list of bad service attributes:

1. Rude
2. Little eye contact
3. Passes the buck
4. Makes excuses
5. Uninterested in his or her job
6. Blames policy or another department
7. Uses phrases like, "I don't get paid enough to deal with that"
8. No follow-up
9. Inconsistent
10. Poor communication skills

Once again, there is probably some overlap between your list and ours. Though you have listed things that you personally associate with bad service, some very common attributes repeatedly emerge when people are asked to complete this exercise. Let's take an example: Item 9, inconsistent service. Inconsistency leads to poor quality, unpredictable service, and sometimes even the dissolution of an organization. The former company People Express Airlines serves as a notorious example of inconsistent service. People Express Airlines started in 1981 and in two years was the fastest-growing airline in the country, with its signature low-cost fares and limited service. In 1985, two years after its peak, the airline started to crumble due to overexpansion, sharp competition, and overwhelmed operations. In short, the company was unable to manage its growth properly, and though customers didn't expect five-star service since they were paying such low prices, they still expected a certain level of consistency in the service they were receiving. It just wasn't there, and People Express Airlines was eventually bought out by Continental.

The two lists of good and bad service paint a general picture of the service extremes. It is a powerful portrait that reminds us of those things we should be doing and those things we shouldn't be doing in our own jobs in higher education. That brings us to the next critical step: directly applying the lessons of good and bad service to our organizations.

Step 4: Your Department's Service Delivery

In Exercise 4, think about your own office on campus. Whether you are a staff member, manager, or director, you are part of a team. Your office comprises a team of people who make up a group, department, or perhaps a division. Your team may not necessarily deliver a service to students directly or exclusively. Perhaps your office provides a service to other staff members or different departments within your institution. Regardless of the service your team delivers (and whomever it provides that service to), in Exercise 4, write down all of the words that describe your team's service delivery. Your perceptions and opinions are what count in this exercise. Of course, there are good days and there are bad days, but in general and on average, how would you describe your department's service delivery? To help you get started, think about the services you provide and refer back to the lists you made describing both good and bad service. Feel free to use any of the attributes from either of those lists, or to add new ideas or thoughts that come to your mind now that you are applying the exercise to your own work environment. Remember, the list should not describe any one staff member's service delivery; rather, describe service delivery for your entire team.

EXERCISE 4 **My Department/Division Customer Service Delivery**

Most of us have to take a few moments to really think about what everyone on our team does, what we provide as a group, and what among all these activities qualifies as service delivery. It is also tempting to focus on the highs and lows of service delivery simply because we remember those instances with greater clarity. Exercise 4 is a collective description of service delivery by your entire team, those individuals with whom you work most closely on a daily basis.

Perhaps you outlined several strengths that describe your office. For example, the advisors from the College of Health Sciences mentioned at the beginning of the chapter have been very intentional about their service delivery. The advising office has even complemented service training with technical tools to quickly and accurately outline degree paths for its students. On the other hand, you may have listed some areas for improvement. Most of us have seen anxious students who are greeted with a lackluster "Next," after waiting in a long line at a student accounts office. This can perpetuate a bad service cycle, a poor reputation for the office, and negative word of mouth, as students talk to each other about the poor service they received. However you described your office in Exercise 4, you have built a description of customer service delivery for your team based on your perceptions. You are part of that team and influence the service the team delivers, so the description also reflects your personal service delivery to some degree. But now it's time to get more direct and to the ultimate point of application.

Step 5: Your Service Delivery

The most difficult (yet most useful) exercise is to assess ourselves. That is the ultimate application. It is easy for us to think about good and bad service experiences when we are on the receiving end, since we are evaluating other people. It is also easy to construct general lists, as we did in Exercises 2 and 3. Those exercises were important, though, because we human beings naturally "warm up" for more detailed work by first thinking about general, big-picture descriptions. Exercise 4 was a little closer to home. You are included in the team you described, so it becomes a little more personalized. Still, when you describe the team, you are blended into a collective group picture of service delivery.

In Exercise 5, we now move from the general to the very specific—describing your personal service delivery attributes. This is a difficult exercise to complete objectively. Most of us are loathe to confront our weaknesses, or in the case of service delivery, those things that could stand improvement. Some people on the other end of the scale are modest and feel awkward describing their strengths. Whatever the case, if you find it difficult to describe your own service delivery objectively in Exercise 5—good, bad, or anything in between—then think about how other people would describe you. Start building your portrait from there.

EXERCISE 5
My Personal Service Delivery

Strengths   Respond to emails quickly

Your personal service delivery assessment will have two critical outcomes. First, reflective practitioners are more effective practitioners. Exercise 5 is reflective, but it is meant to spur you to action. By taking the time to assess (and write down) your own service attributes honestly, you become conscious of those things you do well and those that, perhaps, need some attention. It now becomes more difficult to go through each day on autopilot. By creating a list of your strengths and weaknesses in Exercise 5, you build a picture of your personal service delivery attributes into your short-term memory. If something is in your short-term memory, you will begin to consciously recognize and reinforce your strengths while flagging weaknesses as they occur in real time.

A second critical outcome of Exercise 5 actually relates to Exercise 4. You now have a mechanism with which to compare a description of your team's service delivery to your personal service delivery. This is important, because it can give you a sense of where you are with respect to your colleagues. For example, if you describe yourself very similarly to your department, then it is probably an indication that you are aligned with other staff. You probably also perceive the department in much the same way as your colleagues and manager. In organizational speak, you are on the same page with the team. If you described yourself more generously than you did the department, it may be time to figure out whether you are judging others too harshly or giving yourself too much credit. Finally, if you described the department more favorably than you did yourself, perhaps you are not giving yourself enough credit? Maybe you need to give yourself time as you master more aspects of your job? Whatever the results—and whatever the reasons for the results—it can be an eye-opening experience when we compare our assessments of self with that of the team.

Defining Service Excellence Summary

People skills are the critical ingredient of service success, including in higher education environments. Staff members with strong people skills are better able to assess customers and avoid the dangers of projecting such customer service killers as a negative attitude or unfriendliness. Employees with strong people skills are able to pick up cues and thus interpret and read what the customer expects and how the customer best receives and accepts service.

Your institution and office may already provide top-notch service and enjoy a well-deserved reputation for excellent service. Still, by completing the exercises in this chapter and the coming ones, you can retain that reputation and continue producing outstanding results. Common sense will continue to be common practice for you.

Remember, it is possible, through training and coaching, to turn every bad attribute into a good attribute that strengthens service. Every person, regardless of job experience, personal background, or personality, can learn how to deliver better service. Training, coaching, and education can help anyone. In higher education, our offices are usually open to training and education because that is our business. Investment in the soft skills will take service to the next level.

The road to excellent service really does start with defining it. The process of examining yourself and your team through the lens of good and bad service is the best way to set the foundation for excellent service delivery. This awareness will lead to application—but there is more to do. We must understand ourselves but also our customers, which is the topic of Chapter 2.

Chapter 1 Takeaways

- Soft skills are key to effective service delivery.
- Good service delivery is defined by the commonsense things we should do when delivering a service.
- Bad service delivery is defined by the commonsense things we should not do when delivering a service.
- The highest levels of service are achieved when department and individual staff service delivery practices are aligned with excellent service attributes.

EXTERNAL CUSTOMER SERVICE

Colleges and universities are in the service business. Whether those we help are students, parents, faculty, accrediting agency officials, or even other offices across campus, we are in the business of serving others. The arguments about whether someone is a customer or a client—or neither—may be the subject of philosophical debate across some campuses, but as a practical matter, any institution can benefit from implementing concepts and ideas associated with "customer service" or the "customer." Customers are the driving force behind any successful organization. Successful campuses, therefore, depend on capable professionals who understand their customers. Building a customer profile is a critical step toward this end.

Customers come to us from varied backgrounds and experiences—they are multidimensional. They also have different needs and expectations. The same customer may even have different needs and expectations at different times. Consider a senior student who visits the registrar's office on your campus in the fall semester to determine whether there are extra seats available in a much-sought-after class. Later in the semester, this same student also visits the office to request a transcript. The same student has two different purposes during these two different visits, which means each service request is associated with different needs and expectations. In the earlier visit, the student, in her next to last semester, needs to enroll in a class for credit toward graduation. She also is unable to take the class next semester due to a schedule conflict with some personal responsibilities. The trip to the registrar's office is important because its outcome has implications for her ability to graduate on time. The second visit seems less time critical but may be equally important—say the student wants to verify that a mistake has been corrected because she wants to submit a packet (including transcripts) to a prospective employer. From the customer's perspective, then, the two visits are different, even if they both are standard requests made of office personnel. A staff member who conveys a sense of caring and follow-through during either visit enhances the student's experience.

Different customers with changing needs and expectations give rise to new and sometimes challenging service situations. Countless variables influence a given situation, which makes controlling a service experience difficult for employees who lack service training and knowledge. A good step to build service knowledge is to create a customer profile for those you serve. An effective profile provides a foundation to help service providers manage the complex array of circumstances, needs, and expectations of their various customers. The magic of a customer profile is that neither the actual profile nor the process required to build it is complex, yet it can help you navigate the most difficult of circumstances so that you may provide effective service to your customers.

The Three External Customer Profile Questions

Figure 2.1 presents a three-step approach, or framework, to build an external customer profile. An external customer profile, for an individual or a group, is built by asking three simple questions, in sequential order:

- Who are they?
- What do they want?
- How have they changed?

The framework in Figure 2.1 is easy to use, easy to remember, and easy to share with others. Customer profiles can help an entire office staff better understand its customers, which in turn enables excellent customer service. But it is not only the top executives or administrators in a division or department who are knowledgeable about customers or providing excellent service to them. The answers to all three questions in the framework emerge by gathering and using team input. In fact, employees and staff working on the front lines often know most about the office's customers and how to meet their needs and expectations. The vice president (VP) of student life may be responsible for providing an institutional profile of the student residents, but it is the resident advisors (RAs) who are in contact with the students every day. A key step, then, would be for the VP to work with the RAs when constructing a customer profile to better describe the institution's current and prospective students.

There are many different ways to approach the three questions in the framework, and we will walk you through some exercises to apply the questions as they pertain to your customers. At the end of the day, you know your customers best. The framework is just an organized guide to bring your knowledge about your customers. The benefit of building a comprehensive customer profile goes

Step 1
Who Are They?

Step 2
What Do They Want?

Step 3
How Have They Changed?

Figure 2.1   The Three-Step Approach to Understand External Customers.

beyond immediate use; it will help you adapt to your customers' changing needs and expectations. This, in turn, will enable you to provide the best possible service to those who need your help.

Step 1: Who Are They?

Before we address this first question, let's define what we mean by an *external customer*. As a higher education professional, you can identify several different types of individuals to whom you provide service daily, weekly, or even yearly. The first people you think of probably are not employed by your institution—students and parents immediately come to mind. Students and parents seem to align with the idea of customer because they pay tuition, fees, room and board, and other expenses to your institution. They are buying something, and we normally describe people buying something as customers. In exchange for their money, students receive an education, perhaps housing, and many other direct and indirect benefits from your college or university. Students and parents are definitely external customers.

In higher education, external customers extend beyond students and parents, however. Your customers also may be other employees at your institution. These are employees with whom you do not work regularly, and they are usually not part of your immediate department or division. They come to your office from time to time to receive a service rather than to help you deliver a service. Faculty and administrators from various offices across campus are prime examples. Let's assume you work in human resources (HR), and a faculty member comes to your office to update a personnel form. This faculty member would be an external customer to HR. In this instance, the faculty member comes from outside your immediate team and is looking to your office for help this one-time (or maybe once-a-semester) update.

An *external customer* is anyone who comes from outside of your immediate office for help. These external customers may or may not be from your campus. A technology or computing center on a campus primarily serves external customers who also work on campus and range from individual faculty and staff to entire departments. External customers also include alumni, legislators, guests at sporting or cultural events, and a host of other people and groups. Contrast this with coworkers, managers, and directors in your administrative department with whom you interact regularly and who are part of your immediate team. These are your *internal customers*, and we discuss this type of customer at length in Chapter 3. Table 2.1 provides two guidelines that help describe external customers.

The first application question for anyone interested in providing great service is: "Who are my external customers?" Let's apply this question to higher education but also to other industries, just to generate additional ideas. Table 2.2 shows a list of external customers from three different organizations:

TABLE 2.1
Guidelines Describing External Customers
1. Any person or organization, from outside your institution, who comes to you for a service or some kind of help.
2. Any person or group from within your institution who is from outside of your immediate department or division, but relies on you to provide a service (as opposed to working with you to help deliver a service).

TABLE 2.2		
Example External Customers		
Metropolitan Hospital	Las Vegas Hotel & Casino	University Admissions Office
• Patients • Expectant mothers • Elderly patients • Heart patients • Insurance companies • Pharmacies • Patients' families	• Vacationers • Convention attendees • Business travelers • International travelers • Visiting family of the local population	• Students • In-state students • Out-of-state students • International students • Parents • Helicopter parents • Snowplow parents

a metropolitan hospital, a Las Vegas hotel and casino, and a university admissions office. Examples from outside of higher education provide a fresh perspective and reinforce the idea that customer service is a universal concept that can be applied to many different organizations.

The metropolitan hospital is a good example of the various external customers that an organization may serve in its day-to-day operations. Although a hospital's primary customers are patients, there is no one standard patient. There are many types of patients who may range from expectant mothers to heart surgery recipients. Patients may be young or elderly. They may be in and out in one day, or they may be admitted for a substantial amount of time. A hospital's external customers come from many different circumstances and with many different needs. The hospital's external customers are not limited solely to patients. Insurance companies, pharmacies, clergy, and families are also important external customers with their own sets of needs. Insurance companies and pharmacies are organizations that rely on the hospital to do their work. Clergy frequently find themselves at a hospital in support of both patients and families, using the hospital's space and facilities for private prayer and meetings. Families that accompany their loved ones to a hospital interact with staff and also should be thought of as external customers, aside from the fact that they actually may be the people paying the hospital bills for their loved ones. To provide adequate customer service, the hospital must acknowledge and serve each of these external customers by meeting each one's multiple and varied needs.

Table 2.2 shows another example outside of higher education—a Las Vegas hotel and casino. Hotels and casinos find themselves serving many different external customers. Vacationers may include a couple who drives from California to Nevada for the weekend, an entire wedding party, or international travelers. Increasingly, Las Vegas is considered a family destination; some hotels include attractions such as theaters, large pools, circuses, and animals. The city is host to a multitude of business travelers and conventioneers, so hotels and casinos have ample meeting space and offer a variety of business services. Las Vegas hotels and casinos have done a very good job meeting the needs of their very diverse clientele.

Let's return to higher education and get a little more specific about the different external customers whom an admissions office may serve, as shown in Table 2.2. Many different types of students may be found on a campus today: in-state students, out-of-state students, international students, and many more. These students, all from various backgrounds, have different needs before they are admitted, after they have been accepted, and once they arrive. Then, throughout their time as undergraduates, their needs continue to change, right up until graduation. Some will even become graduate students, which means they will come to the admissions office with yet a different set of needs from those of their undergraduate years. For admissions professionals, serving students is only part of the story, because there are several other very demanding external customer groups, including parents. Not only are many parents financing their children's educations, but they also are very involved in their children's lives. Stories abound about helicopter parents who hover over their children well into their adulthood. Most recently the term *snowplow parents* has emerged. These parents take their children's future into their own hands, plowing and clearing the path of any obstacles. The skills that admissions staff need to handle helicopter and snowplow parents requires a delicate balance between meeting service needs and making sure the work of the institution moves forward without too much disruption from high-maintenance external customers.

Now that you are familiar with examples of external customers inside and outside of your institution, it is time to start building your own external customer profile. This is application in action. Exercise 6 asks you to list five external customers. In making this list, you will address the first question in the customer profile framework: "Who are your external customers?" Think about your campus and your office specifically. Who are the individuals or groups to whom you provide service that you would call "external customers?" Write down five of those external customers in Exercise 6.

EXERCISE 6
List Five External Customers (Who Are They?)

1. _Evangelical churches_

2. _Christian colleges (adult programs)_

3. _____

4. _____

5. _____

Step 2: What Do They Want?

You now know who your external customers are, so the second question in the three-step framework is, "What do they want?" Overwhelmingly, in any interaction with a service provider, individuals want to have a quality customer service experience. Michael Silverstein and Neil Fiske, in their influential book, *Trading Up*, state that customers want quality and are willing to "trade up" for better customer service. The authors describe how customers seek quality and how they want an experience to accompany that quality. Silverstein and Fiske created a ladder of benefits to help service providers better understand what is meant by a quality experience—one that will take service to a new level. Organizations provide three different types of experiences: technical, functional, and emotional. A memorable service exchange integrates all three types of experiences. A freshmen student who seeks counseling for challenges with a roommate may see a counselor who knows how to ask a series of questions to assess the problem (technical), but the solution to the problem has to be crafted within the broader context of the student's personal and academic life (functional) so that the advice is applicable to the student and doesn't seem to be just a canned list of suggestions. Furthermore, the student wants to feel like the counselor cares about her problem to the extent that the exchange ends with the freshman feeling as if she can come back anytime, for any reason (emotional).

Joseph Pines and James Gilmore affirm the importance of providing an experience for customers in *The Experience Economy*. They also created a ladder of experiences and concluded that even for organizations that provide a tangible product, what matters is when customers feel like they are receiving a true experience. The experience is at the top of their ladder. Parents, for example, spend hundreds of dollars at national and local pizza restaurants to provide their children with a perceived experience that goes beyond just buying pizza and having the party at home. We have adapted Pines and Gilmore's experience ladder to higher education, as shown in Figure 2.2. The figure shows three different levels of service that higher education customers may receive: (a) basics, (b) services, and (c) experiences. The basics are really the bare minimum your office might do to satisfy the customer. In some ways, they attend to only the technical needs of any given situation.

Applying the Service Experience to Higher Education

Let's say Rebecca, an entering freshman at your institution, is in the Parking Service Office purchasing her first parking permit. If the front desk employee simply charges Rebecca's credit card in the most efficient way possible and sends her on her way with a permit, the technical requirement is met and Rebecca has received a *basic* experience.

The second level of the experience ladder is that of *services*. In service experiences, staff members deliver more than just the basics; they enhance a situation by providing additional benefits or functionality to the customer. If we return to Rebecca's experience of purchasing a parking permit, our front desk employee could move up the experience ladder, to the *service* level, by offering an additional service. Perhaps our staff member can offer Rebecca a map of the campus parking lots and point out where student parking is located throughout the campus. The top level of the experience ladder is delivering an *experience* to the customer. An experience is really about creating a memorable moment, one from which the customer comes away with positive feelings and reactions and even an emotional connection. The way to create this experience and emotional

Figure 2.2 The Experience Ladder for Higher Education Customers.
Note: Adapted and revised for application to higher education. Original conception from Pines and Gilmore's initial work in *The Experience Economy*, 1999.

connection is by customizing the service. These are the experiences that build relationships and compel the customer to say good things about your department or your institution. At the service level, Rebecca received a map with all of the student parking locations throughout campus. The staff member could create an experience for Rebecca not only by giving her a map of the campus but by then asking her about her class schedule. Our staff member can advise Rebecca about the best places and times to park, given her course times and the location of her classes. Of course, the staff member smiles and takes a genuine interest in helping Rebecca during this entire time, which is an application of the good service skills from Chapter 1. Rebecca will come away from her Parking Service Office visit with helpful information that she feels was customized and delivered to her personally—she is leaving with a true experience, which goes beyond merely receiving a service.

The parking permit scenario is just one example of the many experiences students, parents, or other external customers may encounter on a college or university campus. But let's briefly look once again outside of higher education at a couple of other examples: Starbucks and Apple. These two cultural icons have excelled at creating an experience for their customers. Starbucks is one of the most popular suppliers of quality coffee and other specialty drinks. One only has to walk into a Starbucks to realize there is much more going on than coffee sales—Starbucks provides an experience for its many different customers. Businessmen and women, student study groups, stay-at-home moms, and many others enjoy the complimentary wireless access and the dynamism of a public meeting space. We even know doctoral students who have made Starbucks their home away from home. Joseph Michelli captured the Starbucks "recipe" for service in the book *The Starbucks Experience: 5 Principles for Turning Ordinary into Extraordinary*. These principles include such things as "Make It Your Own," "Surprise and Delight," and "Everything Matters." These exemplify creating the customer experience, such as taking ownership of a situation, engaging with and forming connections with others, and ensuring quality every step of the way.

Apple is another example of a company that provides much more than meets the eye. Apple creates an emotional connection between its products and users, which moves them up the experience ladder. Walter Isaacson documents how Steve Jobs, Apple's late CEO, was obsessively attuned to every single feature, component, shape, color, and feel of every Apple product. Jobs recognized that Apple customers wanted and expected a certain elegant simplicity in every aspect, even the packaging. By paying attention to all of these details, and then adding exceptional customer service, Apple delivers a multidimensional experience to its customers, who truly feel affection for their iPhone, iPad, or MacBook Air. In *The Mind Map*, Tony Buzan asserts that our brains make pathways and connections that touch on an emotional and logical level when we experience something with our senses. It is impossible to avoid the emotional experiences the brain automatically creates as a result of these experiences, which affect future purchase and service decisions. Apple creates, in both its products and services, experiences that form these emotional connections. This is why Apple customers are some of the most loyal you can find.

The Parking Service Office provides an administrative example, as applied to higher education, of the experience principles that distinguish standout organizations or offices. These principles also apply to the academic side of the house. The evolution of distance education delivery neatly demonstrates how institutions have progressed up the experience ladder in this area. In the not too distant past, if students wanted to take a distance education class, they could call a college or university, fill out a form, and order a class to take from home. A few weeks later, a package would arrive in the mail with books, handouts, and a bulky video cassette tape. Students would load the video onto a videocassette recorder, watch the professor lecture, complete the assignments, mail all of the materials back to the institution, and receive a grade. At this point, distance education was primarily fulfilling a basic need (bottom of the experience ladder). There were limited services and personal interactions. As the demand for distance education increased, so did students' desire for additional services. These students wanted to receive the same kind of functional support services that were available on a brick-and-mortar campus, such as advising or tutoring. Institutions answered by creating portals for these services or assigning personal advisors. With the addition of these benefits, distance education had risen to the second step of the experience ladder, services. As time progressed, though, even with comparable services, distance education students still desired more in-depth connectivity. Student-to-faculty or peer-to-peer interactions were essential if online course delivery was to move beyond a service and advance to the experience level of the ladder. Distance education providers have answered this desire by integrating means for collaborating with other students in chat rooms, e-mail, or other synchronous or asynchronous mediums. Today, online tools also provide more real-time interaction opportunities with instructors, even though student and instructor are in two different places. Some entirely online institutions, such as Western Governors University (WGU), pride themselves on the experiences their students receive. WGU has both course and subject matter mentors who advise students and guide them through their individualized programs. WGU administration has described how touching their graduation ceremonies are when students meet each other and their mentors in person for the first time. The human connection that takes place during the ceremonies has helped move WGU online education closer to an experience for students.

It is easy to see from examples inside and outside of higher education that what customers really want is an experience. Most of the time customers do not consciously seek out an experience, yet they will remember their perceptions of whether that experience was good or bad. Their perceptions about you, your office, and even your institution will be based on their feelings and memories. Your ability to provide a potent combination of technical, functional, and emotional interactions will determine how far up the experience ladder you take your customers and their recollection of the service they received from your office.

Providing a Service Experience to Your Customers

One of the most powerful ways to figure out what experience will resonate most with your customers is to put yourself in the role of the customer. If you go back to Exercise 6 and review the list of external customers you generated, a very important question arises: What are some things you can do to provide an experience for these customers? Reflect on your own office and what it provides—or should provide—to external customers. Think about good service delivery principles. Remember, services that deliver a combination of technical, functional, and emotional benefits are at the top of the experience ladder in Figure 2.2. With all of this information in mind, complete Exercise 7 by listing five things you can do to provide an experience to your customers.

EXERCISE 7
List Five Ways Your Office Can Provide Customers "What They Want"

1. _____

2. _____

3. _____

4. _____

5. _____

Just as we have saved our lists of good and bad service attributes from numerous seminars, courses, and initiatives, we have also inventoried what different service providers (including higher education professionals) have told us makes the difference between delivering a basic service versus delivering an experience. Here are a few items to compare with your list in Exercise 7:

1. Take time to listen so that you understand the customer's need—this will allow you to "customize" a service solution.
2. Exhibit professionalism at all times, with all customers.
3. Don't leave your customer's concerns to others; take responsibility to follow up and resolve a situation.
4. Work efficiently, but always maintain that "connection" with the customer, whether over the phone or in person.
5. Seek service training and education for yourself.

Customers are all different, but, at the same time, they are very much the same. Everyone wants to be treated as unique and special. That is why it is important to be a good listener, so customers can receive a solution they feel is unique to them, in technical, functional, and emotional terms. Some of the items on the list reinforce the attributes of good service delivery discussed in Chapter 1, but perhaps most important is that we must, as service providers, constantly grow and educate ourselves (Item 5). This is almost second nature to higher education professionals, since we are in the business of helping others receive education, training, and growth. But we still need to make sure we are doing all we can to create these same opportunities for ourselves.

Now that we know who they are and what they want, there is still one more question to answer that will help us deliver excellent external customer service and complete the three-step approach shown in Figure 2.1.

Step 3: How Have They Changed?

Imagine that you have been an employee in the registrar's office at your institution for 20 years. Are the students you assist today similar to those of the past? As you think about the students you have served even over the last five years, you probably have observed tremendous changes. Students, parents, and staff members from other departments have all been influenced by large social and technological shifts in our culture. In turn, these shifts have implications on people's wants, needs, and expectations and, therefore, influence how you interact with and provide service to your specific customers in higher education.

Several social changes have occurred over time. Our college campuses are much more diverse than in years past. Most campuses have seen an increase in the racial/ethnic composition of students, faculty, and staff. Social changes have hit other aspects of today's college students. International student demand for higher education in the United States is stronger than ever, and these students have unique needs that can be quite different from domestic students' needs. Numerous media accounts describe the trend among first-generation students who are still living with their families while also working to help ends meet. Veteran students are yet another group with unique needs that student affairs professionals are working to address. Most recently, the emergence of undocumented students has added to the diverse mix of students and needs that fill our campuses. The social changes do not stop there, however, because students come from all different age groups. It is not uncommon to hear a college president announce at a commencement ceremony the youngest graduate to be age 18 and the oldest to be 80. Indeed, adult learners, those typically 24 years old and older, are commonplace on our campuses today. These students may be veterans, individuals who have left and are returning to school, or from a range of different circumstances. The needs of an adult learner vary from those of an 18-year-old coming straight from high school, or what we usually refer to as the traditional student. Traditional students may want more socialization and a typical college schedule, whereas adult learners may need flexible class hours, locations, and student services availability. There are also commuter and residential students, special needs students, and transfer students. Really, each student is diverse in his or her own way, meaning that new and unique needs are also on the rise.

Technology and Customer Changes

Technological changes have also influenced how our customers have changed. Today's customer is much more technologically savvy. With advances in Internet communications and electronic devices, we can access information quickly and even compare someone's proposed solution against answers in cyberspace. In addition, our smartphones allow us to find a location, a bank balance, or any other bit of information almost immediately. Because our customers have the same ability, they also expect immediate answers. However, just because our customers are expecting an immediate response does not mean that it is always wise to provide one at a moment's notice; rather, it means that we should be mindful of "have it now" customer expectations and learn to manage them using good service skills.

Managing customer expectations in a world of high connectivity and immediate information access has additional challenges. Suddenly, every customer becomes an expert. Students may come to us already knowing a great deal. They have online access to tuition balance and payment information or class enrollment numbers. This information gold mine may be accompanied by a sense of confidence—or, in too many cases, overconfidence. Your customers may feel like they already have answers to questions; they simply want confirmation. But what they often lack is knowledge of how one piece of information may be related to other pieces. A student may see that he or she is the third person on the waiting list for a very popular class, so the student is confident about the chances for securing enrollment. What this student may not know is that the class was recently moved to a smaller room, so what would normally be true (the student will get in) is now unlikely. Nonetheless, the student has now formed an expectation, perhaps based on experience and access to online information, but he or she still lacks additional information and context that you as the professional service provider have. In countless situations where customer access to information shapes expectations, service delivery takes on a whole new dimension. You now have to manage relationships and expectations with customers who think they have your level of information and expertise, even though they may not.

Customer Involvement

Customer management is not only more important today because of information availability—customers simply want to be more involved when they purchase an experience, either for themselves or someone else. Take the case of parents at any new student orientation. If you work in an orientation office, you know that there are now entire tracks of orientation devoted specifically to parents: answering their questions, calming their fears, and giving them most of the same information their student is receiving. It may not stop there; parents today want to be in the room as the student registers for classes, which isn't always productive or best for the student. Still, the desires (and sometimes directives) of parents as external customers merit consideration. Parents are well-intentioned, and they are proactive in the academic lives of their children. They want their children to succeed and will do everything in their power to ensure that success. From the first time they look at your website to helping their children move into the residence halls, parents are involved in every step of the selection and matriculation process. Once school begins, they commonly keep tabs on their children's progress to verify that all is well. FERPA, the Family Educational Rights and Privacy Act, which protects student records and allows students to restrict access, is often the first barrier parents confront. Many parents ensure that their student authorizes the release of information directly to them or even sometimes require their son or daughter to hand over the login and password to his or her student account. If there are any hiccups along the way, parents are often the first to voice a complaint. In many cases, they are paying for their student's tuition, so they expect to receive a high level of service and want to be informed of their student's progress. As a higher education professional, your conscious awareness of these expectations and parental peculiarities will help you delicately but assertively serve these demanding customers.

Whatever your job in higher education, it is very likely that your customers have changed, in one way or another, over the years. Look at the list of the five customers you created at the beginning of the chapter. Is there a difference in age among your customers? Do they come from different areas of the country or even of the globe? Do they have access to technology? Are they more involved or more demanding? If you answered *yes* to any of these questions, then your customers have definitely changed—and, before you know it, they will change again, just when you have finished fine-tuning your service to meet all of their demands!

External Customer Service Summary

The value of completing the three-step approach is that it generates information and knowledge about your customers. The more you know about your customers, the better you are able to adjust to their needs and wants, given their unique backgrounds and expectations. Specifically, you should now have a customer profile of (a) who your customers are, (b) what they want, and (c) how they have changed. This profile, along with the service delivery attributes you defined in Chapter 1, can help you take service delivery to a whole new level—to the top of the experience ladder.

Chapter 2 Takeaways

- An external customer is anyone who comes from outside of your immediate office for help. These external customers may or may not be from your campus.
- If you answer the question "Who Are They?" you will be able to identify the different types of customers you serve.
- If you answer the question "What Do They Want?" you will be able to meet the needs, wants, and desires of the different customers you serve.
- If you answer the question "How Have They Changed?" you will be able to anticipate the emerging needs, wants, and desires of the different customers you serve.

3

INTERNAL CUSTOMER SERVICE

After a lengthy search process, the College of Sciences at a large research institution had found a new assistant professor for the physics department. Marcia, the college's business manager, was tasked with completing the hiring process before the fall semester, which required her to work with colleagues in Human Resources and the Budget Office. Marcia will have to work closely with these two departments over the next several years, as hiring in the college is projected to ramp up significantly. Teresa, the HR manager, is responsible for ensuring that the search and hiring process is conducted according to strict criteria. Marcia and Teresa have been in constant communication to ensure that all of the proper paperwork is filled out and all of the criteria to execute the hire are completed according to university guidelines. Marcia and Teresa have been responsive to each other and have developed a strong working relationship.

The last step in the hiring process is to complete a line item adjustment in the budget to ensure that the funds are allocated to the appropriate account for the new hire. Joe is the budget analyst who approves and makes changes to the financial accounts. The interaction between Joe and Marcia stands in contrast to the relationship Marcia and Teresa have established. Marcia has e-mailed Joe, requesting the adjustment, but three days have passed and she has not received a response. Marcia decides to walk across campus and ask for Joe's help, and finds him busily typing on his keyboard. Marcia clears her throat to signal to Joe that she is there, but he ignores the cue and continues typing. Finally, Marcia speaks up, "Hi, Joe, how are you doing?" Joe turns briefly to acknowledge Marcia, saying, "I'm fine, thanks, but I'm really busy." Joe then turns back to his computer and, while continuing to type, asks Marcia how he can help. Marcia describes the situation and how both she and Teresa need to ensure that the allocation is logged properly. After Marcia stops talking, Joe briefly turns around, apologizes, and says, "I'm sorry, what were you saying?" Marcia is somewhat annoyed but again describes what is needed, stressing how critical Joe's help is to getting the new professor hired. Joe breathes a deep sigh and simply tells Marcia that he is just too busy at this time and will get to it later. He offers no details and does not explain that the vice president of finance has assigned him a large task and expects a quick turnaround. Marcia begins to express her surprise with Joe's curt communication, but he cuts her off in mid-sentence and reminds her again that he is very busy. He turns back to his computer and starts typing once again. Marcia tells Joe a few choice words, which upsets him. Joe is now distracted from his current task and remains unproductive for the remainder of the day. Even more problematic than this initial exchange is that Joe and Marcia have likely entered a vicious cycle of grudges and payback.

The scenario between Joe and Marcia plays out across countless institutions every day. The details may be different, but the results are the same: poor internal customer service. Many of us have no problem giving the external customer the VIP treatment yet find it difficult to extend the same courtesies to those with whom we regularly work and interact. The problem is one of not viewing our coworkers as customers when they are, in fact, *internal customers*. Internal customers are coworkers you team with on a regular basis to deliver a service. Your internal customers most commonly work in your department, but they may also be from your division or another unit across campus if you work with them regularly.

The Critical Role of Internal Customer Service

Organizations that focus on internal customer service find success in many ways: increased employee satisfaction, spillover to external customer satisfaction, and increased profits. In the 1980s, the founder and then-CEO of Southwest Airlines, Herb Kelleher, famously turned the traditional "the customer is always right" adage around by focusing on internal service. Employees, in Kelleher's view, were the priority. Take care of the employees, treat them right, and make sure they are happy. Make sure there is an atmosphere of respect and fun. Each employee is special, and every person should treat every other person in the company as a VIP. This is an inside-out mentality: Take care of the people on the inside (internal customers), and they will be sure to take care of the people on the outside (external customers).

More recently, Zappos, the company that became famous for selling shoes online, also has an inside-out philosophy. In his book *Delivering Happiness*, CEO Tony Hsieh describes how a focus on internal customers created one of the fastest-growing companies in the country. Included in the company's 10 Core Values is "Deliver WOW through service." This WOW factor is specific to both internal and external customers. According to Hsieh, "Whether internally with coworkers or externally with our customers and partners, delivering WOW results in word of mouth. Our philosophy at Zappos is to WOW with service and experience." This mind-set is clearly at play in the Zappos offices, which are open for public and group tours. Visitors see firsthand how innovation and creativity thrive in an environment of mutual respect and positive team spirit. This philosophy seems to be working, with Amazon's $850-million acquisition of Zappos in 2009 and continued growth to date.

Internal customer service takes place in higher education institutions just as it does in businesses like Southwest and Zappos. Like Marcia and Teresa in the hiring scenario at the beginning of the chapter, there are plenty of examples of higher education staff who make internal customer service a priority. But exemplary business organizations have explicitly, publicly, and purposefully promoted the idea of internal customer service as a philosophy and strategy. Higher education institutions are rightly focused on student success, but we rarely hear of institutions that have explicitly stressed the role of internal customer service as a critical strategy to accomplish broader goals. This needs to change.

A campus-wide strategy that identifies internal customer service as a path to institutional success is important, yet implementation of such a strategy starts with each employee. Do you have an accurate understanding of your internal customers? Do you think of your coworkers as customers? A profile can help you understand your internal customers more deeply and what it takes to serve them. An internal customer profile helps define the interdependent relationships in your office, and it will make one thing very clear: Excellent external customer service is achieved through a team of people who deliver excellent internal customer service.

Think for a moment about the people with whom you work. There are undoubtedly individuals on the team whom you look forward to working with. They are your favorites. If one of these people asks you for assistance on any particular issue, you are more than willing to drop what you are doing to help. You treat these coworkers like VIPs and deliver excellent internal customer service to them. On the other hand, there are probably a few individuals you work with whom you would hesitate to help on a moment's notice. You wouldn't be so willing to drop everything just to help them meet one of their deadlines. There may be some baggage in this relationship because you feel they haven't been very responsive to you when you needed help. Imagine how Marcia, our business manager at the beginning of the chapter, would react if Joe suddenly needed help from her. It would not be easy for Marcia—or any of us—to forget how Joe treated her and then respond cheerfully to one of his requests for help. If you wish to turn the tables a bit, ask yourself if your coworkers view you as a favorite. Do they look forward to working with you? Would they drop everything at a moment's notice to help you out? These are important questions to begin asking ourselves as we work to deliver excellent internal customer service within our offices.

The Three Internal Customer Service Profile Questions

To improve internal customer service, you must profile your internal customers by asking a series of questions you can apply to your situation, on your campus, and in your office. Chapter 2 provided an effective three-step approach for gaining insight into your external customers. This same three-step approach, shown in Figure 3.1, may be applied to your internal customers:

Figure 3.1   The Three-Step Approach to Understand Internal Customers.

Most of us have not really thought about applying these questions to our coworkers. Going through this process casts coworkers in an entirely different light. What if Joe, our budget office guru, had asked himself these questions and discovered that Marcia is his internal customer. Absent this revelation, Joe will probably continue to ignore Marcia's request until she has to explain to the dean of her college that the process is stalled because the funds are not yet allocated to the proper account to execute the hire. The dean may end up going to Joe's manager and, of course, Joe will deliver his own version of the story. If Marcia and Joe view each other as internal customers, they can work together to find a solution and avoid an escalation that eventually involves management. That is the power of profiling your internal customers.

Step 1: Who Are They?

Internal customers are colleagues; they are members of the same team. Internal customers work with one another on a regular basis, and it is the productive interdependency between or among them that makes it possible to deliver a service to an external customer. Your internal customers may be colleagues from within your own group, program, department, or institution. An entire department, like the budget office or HR, may be your internal customer. Although your internal customers are by definition from inside your own institution, not all employees from the institution are your internal customers. Faculty and staff go to the recreation center to receive a service rather than to help produce and deliver that service. In this case, faculty and staff who wish to use the campus recreational facilities are external customers to recreation staff—they are not internal customers. Table 3.1 provides four guidelines that help describe internal customers.

The four guidelines lead to the first major question, "Who are my internal customers?" This is a very personalized question. If four people who work for the same department are asked to identify external customers, their lists

TABLE 3.1
Guidelines Describing Internal Customers
1. Colleagues whose contributions you regularly rely on to do your job
2. Colleagues who regularly rely on your contributions to do their jobs
3. Any group or department that you regularly rely on to do your job
4. Any group or department that regularly relies on you to do its job

TABLE 3.2		
Examples of Internal Customers		
Metropolitan Hospital (Nurse Perspective)	**Las Vegas Hotel & Casino** (Front Desk Manager Perspective)	**Financial Aid Office** (Financial Aid Director Perspective)
• Other nurses • Doctors • Administrative staff • Janitorial staff • Physical therapists • Billing department • Ambulance services	• Front desk employees • Catering • Housekeeping • Maintenance • Chefs • Dealers • Floor boss • Dealers • Cocktail waitresses • General manager	• Registrar's office • Media relations • Housing • Veteran's affairs • Associate and assistant financial aid directors • Front-line and processing staff • Admissions director

will look similar. But if these same four people are asked to identify their internal customers, their lists will look different. That is because we all do different jobs, which means the network of colleagues we depend on to do our jobs is not the same. So identifying your internal customers is the first step to delivering excellent service to them.

Table 3.2 shows the internal customers for three different organizations. Some of the organizations may look familiar. The left and middle columns are the same organizations from Table 2.2, in the "Examples of External Customers" exercise. Just as there was value in looking at different types of organizations when examining external customers, there is also value in looking at different organizations when examining internal customers. Asking the question, "Who are my internal customers?" is something all employees should do—whether they work at a Las Vegas hotel and casino or on a university or community college campus.

In Table 3.2, the question "Who are my internal customers?" is asked from the perspective of an individual employee or staff member, such as a nurse, front desk manager, or financial aid director. Creating an internal customer list is an individualized exercise. The results for all three columns listed in Table 3.2 are actual examples professionals have identified as their internal customers.

In the case of the metropolitan hospital, the nurse has many internal customers. She constantly communicates with other nurses, doctors, and physical therapists. The communication effectiveness among internal customers is directly proportional to the quality of care the patients receive. It may seem odd that the nurse also defines the billing department as an internal customer, but some explanation will clarify why the nurse places this department on her list. Patients often have concerns about billing or administrative issues, and the person they feel the most comfortable with is usually the nurse. It is the nurse they see the most. The nurse may not be able to answer patients' billing questions, but if she has a good working relationship with those who can answer these questions, this may help the patients and their families make better-informed decisions.

The front desk manager of a Las Vegas hotel and casino that provided feedback for the questions in Table 3.2 also has many internal customers. Positive relationships between the front desk manager and these internal customers enhance the external customer experience. In addition to identifying front desk employees and the general manager as internal customers, specific departments and individuals also made the list. The front desk is the first place hotel guests turn to when they have housekeeping or even food requests. If the front desk manager identifies the housekeeping and catering departments as internal customers, front desk guest questions or concerns on just about any issue will be addressed quickly and efficiently because of this internal communication network.

A financial aid director has much in common with a nurse and front desk manager in that effective internal customer service results in effective external customer service. The financial aid director works closely with the registrar's office to ensure that aid packages are available to new and returning students. Special issues for resident students and veterans require communications with housing or veteran's affairs. Local newspaper or television inquiries mean the director may need to coordinate with media relations to formulate appropriate responses. Most important, the financial aid director works closely with her own staff, including frontline employees, processing staff, and the associate and assistant financial aid directors. Good internal customer relationships then have a positive impact on the service students receive, in terms of their experience with the financial aid office and an appropriate aid package.

Each list of internal customers in Table 3.2 illustrates the interdependent nature of coworkers and colleagues. The best way to apply the concept of internal customers to your job is to make a list of your own internal customers now that you have seen several examples. In Exercise 8, list five of your internal customers. You may list departments or groups, but you may be able to list individual colleagues by name. The more specific your list, the more likely you will see results applying the concepts of internal customer service.

EXERCISE 8
List Five Internal Customers (Who Are They?)

1. _Faculty_
2. _Provost_
3. _VPs_
4.
5.

Now that you have identified five internal customers, the next step helps you examine their service needs more deeply.

Step 2: What Do They Want?

External customers want a quality customer service experience; internal customers want the same thing. Quality internal customer service is highly sensitive to the quality of relationships between and among coworkers. The quality of these relationships determines how effectively and efficiently people work together to complete the business of the institution. Poet and author Maya Angelou once said, "People may not remember exactly what you did or what you said, but they will always remember how you made them feel." Angelou's insight is at the foundation of creating a positive customer service experience for both external and internal customers. For most of us, this advice is easier to practice with external customers than it is with internal ones. Our internal customers are the people we see weekly or even daily. We are relaxed around our colleagues, and we do not have to put up a front. While finding comfort and acceptance with colleagues may strengthen our professional relationships, it also makes it harder to think of them as customers. How many of us automatically consider the person sitting in the next cubicle as an internal customer who should be on the receiving end of every best customer service practice we can deliver? This is not natural for most of us. The three-step approach in Figure 3.1 consciously embeds this mind-set into our daily interactions and activities with both internal and external customers.

Please revisit your list of internal customers in Exercise 8 ("Who Are They?"). What are some specific things you can do to deliver great service and provide a positive experience to these internal customers? Are there common things that all five of these internal customers want—and that you can provide if you make the conscious effort? These are the types of questions that can help you identify what they want. In Exercise 9, identify five things you can do, practice, or demonstrate to deliver great service to your internal customers. These five things provide the answer to the question "What Do They Want?" You can write down single words, phrases, or even sentences to describe what they want, but you should complete the exercise thinking about your internal customers and what they would say they want from you. None of your answers should depend on anyone else's actions or reactions. The five items should be things you can do and control.

EXERCISE 9
Internal Customers: "What Do They Want?"

1. _Knowledge on assessment_

2. _Accuracy in reporting_

3. _Good relationship_

4. _____

5. _____

Over the last ten years, we have inventoried and compared hundreds of answers that people inside and outside of higher education provided to Exercise 9. No matter how different the internal customers are ("Who Are They?"), the list of items that define "What They Want" is remarkably similar, whether a hotel clerk, a nurse, or a director of student life creates that list. Here is a representative list of characteristics, phrases, and descriptions that capture what professionals across industries say internal customers want:

1. A good listener
2. Helpful
3. Keeps everyone informed (good communicator)
4. Positive attitude
5. Flexible
6. Knowledgeable
7. Will find the answer
8. Honest
9. Owns the problem
10. Shows patience

This list may look very familiar on two counts. First, there is probably overlap between your list and ours. You may have used some different wording, but the ideas are the same. Second, this list looks like the general list of Good Customer Service descriptors (Chapter 1, Exercise 2) and likely captures the Five Ways Your Office Can Provide "What They Want" (Chapter 2, Exercise 7). You may find some minor differences among the lists, and a few items may have made one list but not the others. Item 10, "Shows patience," is a good example. People who have gone through this exercise say it is usually harder to be patient with a coworker than with an external customer. That is why they listed patience as a specific item, as a reminder of its role in internal service delivery. Everyone knows to show restraint with an external customer, but the same applies to internal customers.

Excellent internal customer service and the professional relationships that result from that service improve the likelihood that we will find meaning in our jobs. Most people feel an intrinsic sense of satisfaction from their jobs when they give and receive good internal service. This satisfaction goes beyond money, and it is often the reason higher education professionals choose to work in a campus environment rather than a corporate one.

If you wish to elevate your appreciation of the value of good internal customer service further, your team needs only to complete another exercise: Review the opposite of good internal customer service and list attributes associated with bad internal customer service. The interaction between Marcia and Joe at the beginning of this chapter is just one example of bad customer service. We have all experienced or witnessed bad internal customer service situations. Perhaps during a particularly stressful time, you can actually remember when your service delivery to a colleague was less than optimal. What does poor internal customer service look like? How would you describe "What They Do Not Want?" Here is a list of five negative internal customer service attributes we have gathered over the years:

1. No follow-up
2. Passes the buck (blames others or "the system")
3. Negative attitude
4. Acts as if he or she is doing others a favor
5. Unapproachable

Regardless of whether you work in student affairs, the admissions office, or the library, it is not difficult to identify poor internal customer service. This brief list looks similar to the general list of bad service delivery in Chapter 1, and that is because bad service is bad service, whether we are dealing with internal or external customers.

The good news is that you have now answered the first two questions from the Three-Step Approach shown in Figure 3.1. That means you understand who your internal customers are and what it is that they want. Those are the two key ingredients you need to deliver immediate, quality customer service to your internal customers. Just as with external customers, though, a proactive service provider also anticipates the customer's needs by asking one final question . . .

Step 3: How Have They Changed?

Here is a simple thought experiment. Go back in time two, five, or even ten years. You still work on a college campus in this scenario. The function of your department and the role you fulfill might be a little different from what it is today, but you are still a professional working in higher education. Now imagine that you are in a training session and the facilitator asks you to make a list of your internal customers. She urges you to describe who they are, just as we did in Exercise 8. She asks you to go beyond just identifying their names, by also describing their characteristics, habits, backgrounds, and interests. Now fast-forward to the present. Ask yourself these same questions about your present-day internal customers whom you have already identified in Exercise 8. Compare your past list with your current one. Have your internal customers changed over the years? How do the people on each list look and act? Are there differences in expectations or in the way they communicate? What else has changed about your internal customers? Exercise 10 asks you to list three ways your present-day internal customers have changed compared to the past.

```
┌─────────────────────────────────────────────────────────────┐
│                      EXERCISE 10                              │
│   List Three Ways Your Internal Customers Have Changed        │
├─────────────────────────────────────────────────────────────┤
│  1.  Faculty are more knowledgeble and                        │
│        independent on assessment                              │
│  2.  More heavily burdened (increased enrollment)             │
│                                                               │
│  3.                                                           │
│                                                               │
└─────────────────────────────────────────────────────────────┘
```

The changes you identified may have been related to technology and diversity, similar to the changes you identified for external customers. Yet, serving internal customers who are more technologically savvy and more diverse is somewhat different from serving technologically savvy and diverse external customers. We interact with internal customers more regularly than we do with most external customers. This means that if we wish to communicate with technologically savvy internal customers, we may need to become familiar with technology as well. Some internal customers may prefer to receive e-mails, text messages, or instant messages on their smartphones instead of a telephone call. They may prefer a video call instead of an in-person meeting. This new "connectedness" may be superior to face-to-face meetings and telephone calls in certain situations but inferior to them in others. Texting and e-mailing are what are known as "lean" communication channels because they lack nonverbal cues, and intent is easily misinterpreted. Serving customers effectively means using appropriate communication channels but also gaining a certain level of comfort with various technological media. If your customers change, you may need to change, at least to some degree, as well.

Most higher education institutions pride themselves on educating a diverse student population, and they strive to employ a diverse workforce to match. We work with colleagues and student workers from different cultural backgrounds, races, ethnicities, age groups, and experiences. Excellent internal service makes such diversity a strength rather than a weakness, but just as adaption is needed with new technologies, so, too, is adaption needed to serve diverse internal customers effectively.

Even though internal customers have changed in various ways, much of what they seek from their jobs remains the same. As early as 1941, research began uncovering what people really wanted from their professions: recognition and quality relationships. Frederick Roethlisberger's groundbreaking studies examined employee productivity. His team found that productivity increased when a group of female employees were able to talk to others about their concerns, thoughts, and feelings. The researchers had to learn to listen. In 1968, Frederick Herzberg's *Harvard Business Review* article "One More Time: How Do You Motivate Employees?" found that relationships and the value of the work itself are important forms of rewards that people seek. Marcus Buckingham, in *The One Thing You Need to Know*, confirms that the need for respect in our work relationships is instrumental to long-term success for any employee. The findings of these and subsequent studies confirm that employees in any organization seek recognition, appreciation, interesting work, and positive relationships. Many of these things will materialize when you deliver good internal service, and it is likely that you will receive excellent service in return.

The Internal-External Customer Service Connection

There is a strong relationship between internal and external customer service. Nowhere is this relationship more crucial than in higher education. Departments across campus are heavily dependent on one another to serve students, faculty, and other staff. Consider the level of internal customer service that two different departments must deliver to each other to assist international students (the external customer). Due to the complexities of admitting and matriculating an international student, the Office of Admissions (credential evaluation) and the Office of International Students and Scholars (processing) must be in constant contact. The two offices must exchange information, and staff members across the two departments must keep each other informed of any emerging obstacles that may prevent admission or matriculation. Problems might arise from a federal office with respect to a visa, or perhaps issues with account and payment verification might suddenly crop up. The two offices must be in sync, sharing and exchanging information and communications so the student does not fall through the cracks.

International students bring diversity and cultural awareness to college campuses, and admissions and international student offices play a critical role in making that happen. Talk to a handful of international students and ask them why they chose your institution. You may be surprised to find that international students often pick a particular institution because its administrators were responsive and helpfully resolved requirements and logistics for their study abroad. That is the power of internal customer service in action.

Ultimately, an institution's external customer service is only as good as its internal customer service. Figure 3.2 shows the relationship between internal and external customer service.

A team of people must first provide each other with strong internal service before they can deliver exceptional external customer service. When internal

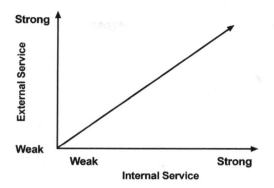

Figure 3.2   Relationship Between Internal and External Customer Service.

customer service is weak, the team is too busy solving its own problems to address the external customer's problems. In addition, internal service problems lead to external service problems, such as providing an external customer with two different answers to the same question. The logical conclusion is that weak internal customer service ultimately leads to weak external service. Fortunately, the opposite is also true: Strong internal customer service ultimately leads to strong external customer service.

In an environment of strong internal service, external customer service becomes an effortless, natural part of the organization. Tim works in the Office of Civic Engagement on his campus. Tim's director has one mantra for supervisors and staff: communicate, communicate, communicate. Tim enjoys being part of a team at the Office of Civic Engagement because its philosophy is that if team members serve each other well, then service to students will follow.

The relationship between internal and external customer service shown in Figure 3.2 always holds true in the long run. It is possible that, for a time, a department delivers strong external customer service even though internal customer service is weak. The problem with this situation is that strong external customer service is not going to last very long. In the long run, weak internal customer service will reach a breaking point, and, like a balloon that fills up with too much air, the previously strong external customer service eventually bursts into nothing.

Internal Customer Service Summary

The three-step approach applies to both internal and external customers:

1. Who Are They?
2. What Do They Want?
3. How Have They Changed?

Answering these three questions within the context of your work environment strengthens your ability to provide excellent internal customer service, which translates into improved teamwork, increased job satisfaction for individual employees, and a more pleasant workplace overall. Institutions that make internal customer service an explicit priority also enhance communication between departments. External customer service problems are often linked to ineffective communication between departments, and it is here where many directors and vice presidents (who lead multiple departments) spend an inordinate amount of time.

Chapter 3 Takeaways

- An internal customer is an individual or group, from your institution, with whom you work to provide a service.
- If you answer the question "Who Are They?" you are able to define the various internal customers you work with and serve.
- If you answer the questions "What Do They Want?" and "How Have They Changed?" you will improve work relationships and communication with your internal customers.
- External customer service is dependent on internal customer service; good internal service precedes good external customer service.

CYCLE OF SERVICE THINKING

Imagine that a prominent alumna of your institution lives across the country. She contacts the alumni relations department to inquire about the upcoming homecoming game. She wishes to attend the game with her family and has, on her own accord, reached out to your department. Here is an opportunity to create a positive relationship with a valued "customer." Our prominent alumna will have an experience with your office, but will it be a good or bad experience? How will she formulate impressions of her alma mater, now that she has been away for 20 years? The answer to these questions is very simple: The experience and the impressions will take shape from initial contact with the alumni relations department all the way to her departure after the game—which may even include her journey home or any subsequent follow-up. The quality of this experience will define the depth and duration of the relationship that develops between the alumna and the institution.

The way to ensure that our alumna has a positive experience is to break down all of the points of contact, or moments, that will shape her experience. Here is a simplified sample of events, or moments, that will shape the experience. First, the initial contact will create the first impression. Is it easy for our alumna or her assistant to get in touch with the alumni relations department? Actually, the department's website might even be the first point of contact. Does the website have easily accessible contact information? Perhaps even more important in this instance, given that homecoming is one of the year's major activities for your department, is whether there is general, updated information about this event on your website. Let's assume that the alumna has her assistant call the department directly, and the assistant is successful in speaking with a coordinator. Is the alumni relations coordinator friendly, professional, and ready to answer questions about homecoming? One hopes the coordinator will not have to transfer the assistant to another department to get some basic questions answered. The department also should be equipped to help with logistical issues: lodging options, obtaining tickets to the game, and any pregame events that may be scheduled. Of course, the homecoming event itself will have a big impact on our alumna and may represent our biggest chance to make sure she has a memorable experience on campus. Perhaps after some initial information gathering, our coordinator might even determine that it is a good idea to honor or recognize our prestigious alumna at halftime.

After speaking to her director and determining that some sort of honor or recognition is appropriate, the coordinator calls the alumna's assistant, thus defining another moment of contact. Whatever other events unfold in this process of communication and contact, anyone who works in alumni relations or development knows that many moments shape an impression and add to the experience of alumni. Those moments define how successful the institution is at cultivating and developing ongoing relationships, which also provides a measure of how effectively your office is performing.

Cycle of Service: A Brief History

The notion of breaking down the customer experience into a sequence of related moments whereby the customer begins to formulate an impression of his or her experience has roots in an idea titled "A Cycle of Service." Karl Albrecht, in his 1985 book, *Service America*, is largely credited with formally identifying the concept of a Cycle of Service. A Cycle of Service is simply a series of moments that, when put together, defines the customer experience. It is useful to give the Cycle of Service a specific name that ties together the series of moments. In the previous example, the alumni relations office might name a Cycle of Service "Alumna Homecoming Visit." The Cycle of Service as a tool and concept applies to higher education environments as much as—if not more than—other industries and organizations. Higher education institutions have always been in the business of providing a service, whether it is instruction, student services, alumni relations, community service, continuing education, or even research. So, the Cycle of Service concept is really a tool to help us analyze our service delivery and ensure that the series of moments that define customer interaction results in a positive, meaningful experience for the customer.

The Cycle of Service as a concept coincided with the explosion of the service economy, which itself gained momentum in the 1980s and 1990s and has now imprinted the indelible seal of "customer service" on every type of organization. It was in the 1980s and 1990s that the United States really began thinking about the idea of service as a source of competitive advantage. Today, service industries are widespread and dominate our economy. Massive insurance and rental car companies will tell you that they are selling a good customer service experience, not insurance or a rental car. In fact, global corporations that we assume make their money selling products are also in the business of delivering services. Manufacturers such as Toyota and BMW may sell automobiles, but they also make a lot of money financing them. The focus on service has encouraged management thinkers, academic experts, and, certainly, managers and employees who are doing the everyday work of their organizations to analyze more critically the events, activities, and processes that shape a customer's service experience.

Though the Cycle of Service concept was formally developed alongside the growth of the service economy, its roots go back even further. The Cycle of Service idea borrows from what is known as the quality movement, which actually focused on products and goods, or manufacturing. In the early and mid-twentieth century, Joseph Juran and Edward Deming developed several ideas and concepts that came to be known as the quality movement. One enduring tool they distilled and popularized is called *process mapping*. The goal of process mapping is to improve efficiency and create improvements in the manufacturing process by articulating the steps in that process. Process mapping is essentially a visual map of a series of steps that occur on a manufacturing line. With each step explicitly identified, management experts were able to take a scientific approach to analyzing these steps; they were able to define what went on during each one and to identify the people working on or influencing each step. This made it possible to identify problem steps, or inefficiencies in certain steps, that may have been holding up the entire process. Sometimes mapping a manufacturing process did not reveal any significant problems, yet organizations that went through the exercise found unanticipated benefits. For example, the process map might provide clues about problems that were about to surface but had been hidden up to this point.

Juran and Deming certainly had their critics, as detractors felt the quality philosophy was actually dehumanizing the work environment, with its relentless focus on process and tasks. In fact, many of the cornerstone ideas that Juran and Deming offered are arguably meant to accommodate the "human side" of the equation. Nonetheless, some of the controversy surrounding process mapping continues today, as opponents view this exercise as an impersonal dictate that values efficiency above people. The value of knowing our history, however, is that we can integrate the strengths of a given approach into our own thinking and simply drop those ideas that are not applicable to our environment.

Process mapping does have value in the service world and has been applied to service delivery via the Cycle of Service concept. In fact, process mapping, via the Cycle of Service, arguably has more potential in a service environment because it is easier to apply and has less technical detail than maps meant to model a manufacturing environment. Simple ideas are always easier to apply.

Moments of Truth

Just as different steps can be defined on a manufacturing line, so, too, can different steps (moments) be defined in a Cycle of Service. In a service interaction, it is useful to define each of the moments that contribute to a Cycle of Service, to the extent possible. Each of these moments is what Jan Carlzon called a "Moment of Truth" in his similarly named book, *Moments of Truth*. A Moment of Truth is an event within a Cycle of Service and is so called because it is at this moment that the customer begins to make decisions or develop impressions about the quality of our service. We must think about it as more than a step (as in manufacturing) and more than an event (e.g., I am simply delivering an impersonal service); it is a moment that begins to define whether our organization will build a lasting relationship predicated on trust and mutual benefit. During every Moment of Truth, an employee or organization in some way comes in contact with the customer. Carlzon once said his company had 50,000 Moments of Truth every day.

A Cycle of Service may comprise three, four, perhaps even ten Moments of Truth. Within every cycle there is one Moment of Truth that is critical in shaping customer perceptions and feelings about his or her experience. This special Moment of Truth is called a Critical Moment of Truth. In the case of colleges and universities, a Critical Moment of Truth may determine whether a customer maintains a relationship with your institution or tells ten other people what a bad experience he or she had on your campus. Well-executed Moments of Truth and Critical Moments produce customer satisfaction and, perhaps more important for the long term, loyalty. Poor execution produces negative customer perceptions, complaints, negative word of mouth, loss of customers, and, ultimately, a damaged reputation.

The best way to ensure that the Critical Moment of Truth is a positive experience for the customer is to make sure that at this specific moment we are meeting or exceeding the customer's standards and expectations. Thus, the final step in a formal Cycle of Service analysis is to define a Standard of Excellence for the Critical Moment of Truth. The Standard of Excellence draws attention to the Critical Moment and confirms that we are taking some action to ensure that the customer has a good experience at this defining moment. The Standard of Excellence is really a service standard to ensure customer satisfaction. Sometimes the Standard of Excellence is a simple action, such as a friendly "Thank you." Sometimes we can even measure the effectiveness of our actions by asking for the customer's feedback or observing the results of our efforts (e.g., Did the "ask" result in a donation to the college?). The template in Table 4.1 summarizes the Cycle of Service and can help you apply this powerful concept to whatever service your office delivers on campus. Our own customers have told us that simple is better, and that the Cycle of Service template in Table 4.1 is an easy way to map activities and events and define Standards of Excellence.

The Cycle of Service template can be applied to any type of organization. In the airline business, for example, three distinct Moments of Truth occur during a customer's trip: (a) customer arrival, (b) inflight, and (c) destination arrival. A Critical Moment of Truth usually emerges once the Moments of Truth are outlined, and from there the Standard of Excellence is often very easy to define. The Cycle of Service can apply to a company providing an oil change or one that delivers over-the-counter hamburgers and fries. Libraries and soup kitchens also deliver services, and the template in Table 4.1 can help each of these organizations strengthen its services and improve customer satisfaction.

TABLE 4.1
Cycle of Service Template

Cycle of Service:

Moments of Truth

1. _____
   _____

2. _____
   _____

3. _____
   _____

4. _____
   _____

Critical Moment

_____

_____

Standard of Excellence

_____

_____

Applying the Cycle of Service to Higher Education

Now that you have read the theory behind the Cycle of Service and seen that it is applicable to all types of organizations, let's return to the world of higher education and provide another example to see how this concept extends beyond the alumni relations office scenario at the beginning of the chapter. Perhaps your region's community college has a beautiful theater on campus that is home to a series of eight plays during the academic year. Many people enjoy the experience of watching a play on a college campus, and it is something most professionals working on a college campus are familiar with. Posters and advertisements are visible across campus, particularly when each production's date nears, so these events are hard to miss.

The theater department is obviously a critical player in ensuring a successful theater season on your campus, so we will go through this exercise as if you worked for the theater department. Clearly, other departments and people are involved in completing a successful theater season, as will soon become obvious. The real key when going through this process, though, is to complete it from the customer's perspective but with your own insight about the college's inner workings.

The first step in the process is to name this Cycle of Service. Let's call this Cycle of Service the *Theater Experience on Campus*. The next step is to define different Moments of Truth. Now, the theater experience is taking place on campus. From a customer perspective, what is the first point of contact whereby an impression might start to form on the night of the play? Actually, before your patrons even walk into the theater, the Cycle of Service begins. People must find parking, so we might do well to designate Parking as the first Moment of Truth. Most of us who work on a college campus have heard a litany of concerns regarding parking: Is there parking? Can I park here without getting a ticket? How do I find parking close to the theater so I don't end up halfway across campus? Will there be directions? A family attending the play might even wonder whether the parking spaces are big enough for large SUVs. Parking may not be the theater department's responsibility, but if the theater department is producing the Cycle of Service template and defining the Moments of Truth, it must define these moments through the eyes of the customer. From a customer standpoint, parking is an important moment in the entire *Theater Experience on Campus*. Without clear directions or communications about parking, our patrons may get to the theater late and miss some of the play, and that might upset them and even taint their actual viewing experience of the play—so parking is, indeed, a reasonable first Moment of Truth.

The next Moment of Truth, after parking, occurs at the ticket office. We will simply call this moment Ticket Office. Some people will buy their tickets from the box office the night of the play. Most people probably buy their tickets online, but they still have to pick them up at the box office. All of this means that people are going to have to stand in line the closer it gets to curtain time. Theaters and box offices structure their lines differently, leading to different customer experiences. Some theaters have multiple windows and require the customer to choose a line. Normally, you follow a process similar to what you would find at a grocery store: first you assess how many people are in each line, and then you try to discern whether the cashier is leisurely or efficient. After you have made these assessments, you choose your line (and for some reason or another, it usually ends up being the slowest line!). Some movie theaters have gotten smart and do not require people to choose a line, because they arrange their lines much like a bank. There is one long line and multiple cashiers. The customer does not know which cashier he or she will get because the next available cashier calls the next customer who is at the front of the line. Studies have shown that this process, called queuing theory, actually decreases customer wait times, which means an enhanced customer experience.

As you can see, there is a lot to a Cycle of Service and the different moments that comprise it. Our patrons have not even watched the play, and already their perceptions and opinions about the service they are buying are forming in conscious and unconscious ways—many of which are not even directly related to watching the play. So what additional moments must we define?

After a customer receives his or her tickets, there are at least five more Moments of Truth: seating in the theater, the actual experience of watching the play, drinks and concessions at intermission, restroom use during intermission and after the play, and the final return to the parking lot. Attending a play is certainly, from the customer's perspective, about the quality of the play, but the Cycle of Service exercise makes it clear that there are a lot of other things that constitute the *Theater Experience on Campus*.

Let's say we have defined all the Moments of Truth related to the *Theater Experience on Campus*. Once all of the Moments of Truth are identified, the task turns to designating a Critical Moment of Truth. It is very easy to identify a Critical Moment of Truth by asking a couple of questions: Which Moment of Truth has the most potential to satisfy customers or drive them away? Have we received complaints or have customers voiced concerns about anything related to any of the moments? In the case of the *Theater Experience on Campus*, the actual "Play-Viewing" Moment of Truth certainly qualifies as a top candidate for the Critical Moment of Truth. For argument's sake, let's go ahead and designate Play-Viewing as the Critical Moment of Truth.

Setting a Service Standard

Now that you have identified Play-Viewing as the Critical Moment of Truth, it is time to set a Standard of Excellence. The Standard of Excellence is really about establishing a service standard to ensure customer satisfaction. Perhaps there were a lot of complaints last season about the sound quality, or disruptions in sound during the play. Whatever the issue, the Standard of Excellence may create a new process or a standard operating procedure. The Standard of Excellence may establish a new measure that we can track, or it may be as simple as defining steps employees must take to ensure that customers' expectations are met at this Critical Moment. The theater department cannot control whether every patron is going to like a particular play, but several possible Standards of Excellence will serve to ensure that the play-viewing experience is set up for success. Listed here are two possible items to include in our Standards of Excellence.

Possible Standards of Excellence for Play-Viewing
- Sound checks will be conducted at least three times, two hours before curtain time.
- A staff member will walk up and down the aisle every 15 minutes to ensure that there is no unnecessary talking or unruly behavior that might disrupt the pleasure of the play-viewing experience for any customer.

Of course, it is entirely possible to take each Moment of Truth and set a corresponding Standard of Excellence. For example, perhaps the facilities department has received numerous complaints about the cleanliness and functionality of the restrooms in the theater building. This seemingly small issue could create a problem for an event that seeks to draw a sophisticated crowd that comes in with high expectations. An effective Standard of Excellence for the Moment of Truth of "restroom use" may simply be that the theater department's administrative assistant sets up a standard practice of calling the facilities department the day before a production to ensure that the restrooms have been inspected and are clear of any problems—simple, yet effective.

Teamwork and Communication

The Cycle of Service also demonstrates that teamwork and cooperation are often at the heart of effective service delivery. If the administrative assistant wants to ensure that clean facilities are available the night of the play, this means communication must occur between two different departments. This would also be true if, the night after a production, the theater department had received numerous complaints about parking. Parking is not the theater department's responsibility, but the department will likely have to relay such messages to the office of public safety on campus to ensure that the problem is addressed.

If you identify a Critical Moment of Truth, it will help you focus on the most important moment that wins the hearts of your customers and increases their loyalty to you because of the excellent service experience they receive from you. From another perspective, identifying the proper Critical Moment of Truth may help you anticipate and avoid specific customer problems that can taint the entire customer experience. The Critical Moment of Truth is the priority and the starting point, but given time and diligence, you can also give the necessary attention to the other Moments of Truth. The significance of providing Standards of Excellence is that there is a large payoff because these standards often define things that are easy to correct or address. In addition, simple standards are easy to communicate to customers and employees.

The example of the *Theater Experience on Campus* provides an excellent illustration of the entire Cycle of Service process. Table 4.2 is a completed template for the *Theater Experience on Campus*. In Table 4.2, a few of the Moments of Truth are combined for illustration purposes, and we have chosen one Standard of Excellence from our previous list as the priority.

Several hints will help you apply the Cycle of Service template to maximize customer satisfaction and loyalty. First, the Cycle of Service template is most useful if it provides enough detail to be meaningful but not so much that it is stifling. Do not define too many Moments of Truth, Critical Moments of Truth, or Standards of Excellence. Within the *Theater Experience on Campus* shown in Table 4.2, there are six Moments of Truth. If you were to identify

---

TABLE 4.2
Theater Experience on Campus

Cycle of Service: Theater Experience on Campus

Moments of Truth

1. Parking

2. Ticket office

3. Seating

4. Play-viewing

5. Intermission (concessions/restroom usage)

6. Return to parking and departure

Critical Moment

Play-viewing

Standard of Excellence

Sound check 3 times, 2 hours before curtain time, to ensure pleasurable sound during play-viewing

twenty Moments of Truth, ten Critical Moments of Truth, and seven Standards of Excellence for each Critical Moment of Truth, the template would be
unwieldy and lose its utility as an improvement service tool. Remember, simple
is most useable; and simple, commonsense ideas lead to hassle-free, excellent
service. A second point to keep in mind is this: Completing the Cycle of Service
template usually requires a group effort. The template will strike the appropriate balance between comprehensiveness and simplicity if different people are
involved in creating it. Individuals often define too many Moments of Truth,
but if a team is involved and the process is properly managed, consensus usually
develops around a reasonable number of Moments of Truth, Critical Moments,
and Standards of Excellence. Finally, and perhaps most important, remember
that any given Moment of Truth may itself be a Cycle of Service, depending
on the customer's perspective. One of our favorite activities in our seminar and
workshop programs is to break participants into groups of three or four and
look at the Cycle of Service template from different customer perspectives, or
even from different departmental perspectives. For example, how might the
alumni relations department fill out a Cycle of Service template for different
alumni: out-of-town alumni, wealthy alumni, local alumni, current graduates,
and so on? In all likelihood, there will be some differences but also some simi-
larities. In the case of the *Theater Experience on Campus*, would the Cycle of
Service template look different if the facilities department, instead of the theater
department, is completing the exercise? The common focus should be on cap-
turing the customer experience no matter who fills out the template, though it
is possible that minor differences in the template will surface depending on who
(individual or department) goes through the Cycle of Service analysis.

Cycles of Internal and External Customer Service

Departments and groups that invest the time it takes to apply the Cycle of Service
template take a big step toward delivering excellent external customer service,
but there is an additional application that is very important—the Cycle of Service might address internal and external service delivery simultaneously. In fact,
internal service challenges are often at the core of our external customer service
challenges. How many institutions do you know where communication between
and among different departments on campus is perfect? Probably not many.
Perfection is an unachievable standard, of course, but how many instances have
you witnessed where miscommunication between departments causes problems
for our external customers? The departments can't seem to align their own processes, and then the customer ends up confused and frustrated. If this seems like
a common problem that plagues your institution, rest assured that it happens
in business, government, and all types of nonprofit organizations. Colleges and

universities are not alone in this regard. The key is for departments to view each other as internal customers.

Let's examine a situation where a faculty member is unable to access his online university account for viewing class rosters and administering grades. The online account contains course information, but the information systems that allow access to this information must match employee personnel data with course information. In this case, then, the faculty member is an external customer to the information technology (IT) department, HR, and the registrar's office because all of these entities house, manipulate, or access information related to the online account. In addition, IT, HR, and the registrar's office all need to work together, so each department is an internal customer of the other two departments.

Additional details of the situation will clarify how important internal coordination is to resolving the faculty member's issue. Imagine it is the end of the semester, and our faculty member tries to log onto his account to assign grades. Unfortunately, an error message pops up with automatic advice to call the IT help desk. The faculty member's anxiety rises as the grade deadline nears, so he hastily calls the help desk per the instructions in the error message. Upon receiving the call, an IT specialist walks through the problem with this important external customer, using excellent service and communication skills. The specialist discovers that the university identification number on the account is incorrect. The specialist starts a work order, but then, after further investigation, realizes that the identification number is incorrect because there are two instructors at the institution with the same name. The computer apparently has confused the two names and duplicated personal information for both employees. This seems to be the crux of the problem, because the identification number for our panicked faculty member is associated with the wrong birthdate and Social Security number, which has only now surfaced and restricted access to the account. The specialist instructs the faculty member to call the registrar's office to address the personal information mix-up, which will then allow IT to correct the problem. The faculty member calls the registrar's office and explains the problem, but is instructed to call HR, since any alteration or reassignment of sensitive employee information that is related to any employee account requires HR approval. The faculty member calls HR and explains the problem. The human resources officer offers the following solution: Call the IT department since the problem involves an online account. After several frustrating days, the faculty member's problem is finally resolved—but only after he misses the deadline for posting grades. As it turns out, the registrar's office never needed to be involved, and this was actually an issue between HR and IT.

Clearly, this faculty member's inquiry into an online account problem could have benefited from a Cycle of Service analysis. This situation may not be exclusive to a faculty member and may happen to any professional employee working on campus. IT, HR, and the registrar all deliver services to employees within their institution, but when effective delivery requires coordination between departments, the departments become internal customers of each other in the process of delivering a service to an external customer. In this situation, the faculty member is an external customer because he is not involved in defining or delivering the service—he is the recipient of the service. Table 4.3 shows how a Cycle of Service analysis would help document this process and create a formal solution.

The *Faculty Account Inquiry* in Table 4.3 has four Moments of Truth. The Critical Moment occurs at the diagnosis stage, primarily because at this stage it becomes apparent that there is some confusion about who needs to be involved to

---

TABLE 4.3
Faculty Account Inquiry

Cycle of Service: Faculty Account Inquiry

Moments of Truth

1. Specialist takes call

2. Specialist diagnoses problem

3. Specialist solves problem, in coordination with any internal customers (other departments)

4. Specialist verifies the problem has been solved to customer's satisfaction, or verifies action steps with customer

Critical Moment

Specialist diagnoses problem

Standard of Excellence

All departments that are potentially involved in the solution are immediately identified and verified BEFORE customer hangs up

help solve the problem. Of course, the IT team will have to take the time to diagnose the types of problems that arise with faculty accounts, and it may be impossible to anticipate every type of problem. Still, identifying those types of problems we have experienced or know about, such as errors in personal information, will help IT identify which internal customers (in this case, HR) must be involved in the solution. In other instances, it may be that IT has to work with the registrar's office but not with HR. Once this step is completed, the Standard of Excellence requires that IT specialists explicitly identify for the customer any internal departments that are needed to solve the particular problem. To achieve this standard, IT may have to circulate a document among all specialists that identifies different departments that are needed to solve specific types of problems.

Cycle of Service Thinking Summary

The Cycle of Service template is a flexible tool that can be applied to situations that cover external and internal customer service delivery. The goal is to improve service delivery and deliver consistent, quality service. The blank template in Table 4.1 may be very simple, but most people begin to unearth service gaps and problems in their organizations by using this practical tool. In reality, it often takes a team of people to identify a Cycle of Service and its many constituent parts. This process can help a team examine its services from a fresh perspective and subsequently improve service delivery and increase customer satisfaction.

Chapter 4 Takeaways

- The Cycle of Service template is an analytically based tool that complements the interpersonal skills higher education professionals need to deliver excellent service.
- Simple is best: Define a manageable number of Moments of Truth, one Critical Moment, and a limited number of Standards of Service Excellence.
- Develop a Cycle of Service through the eyes of the customer but also with your unique knowledge of internal processes.
- Standards of Excellence should be specific, but the ways in which professionals might meet those standards can vary.
- If a Moment of Truth or a Critical Moment of Truth is particularly troublesome, make that moment its own Cycle of Service so you can uncover more detail and get to the real problem.
- It often takes a team of people to create an effective Cycle of Service template and truly solve customer problems.

5

CUSTOMER EXPECTATIONS

Do your internal and external customers expect a positive experience, quick answers, and immediate service? Do they expect you to solve their problems at the drop of a hat? Have their service expectations escalated? You probably answered *yes* to all of these questions, wherever you happen to work on campus. Parents and students expect to be "wowed" during orientation, and they expect advising and counseling services to lead to perfect grades and solve every problem. Alumni returning for basketball and football games expect an incredible weekend. They want to tap the emotional experience of their college days and relive the student life while filtering out the negative memories of parking problems or nosebleed seats.

Internal customers are just as demanding as external customers. Internal customers expect quick answers to their questions. They expect cooperation and communication. They do expect you to drop everything you are doing and take charge of their problems.

External and internal customers expect everything, everywhere, at any time. Are these escalating demands unreasonable? Yes! This is the nature and progression of customer service. What's more, as service providers, we should be working hard to meet these unreasonable expectations. Our goal should be to create an increasingly positive service experience as quickly, efficiently, and memorably as possible. It is not always possible to meet unreasonable customer demands and expectations, and the customer isn't always right. Our job, however, is to make the customer feel right—like he or she received the right service, at the right time, and in the right way.

Technological advancements have fueled escalating customer demands. The Internet allows students and parents to make instantaneous comparisons between your institution and almost any others before they even set foot on campus. Potential and current external customers formulate perceptions and expectations based on institutional websites as they compare majors, programs, residence halls, and all of the attractive photos they see on the sites they visit. In many states, community college students now have access to websites that explain credits that should transfer to a four-year institution, creating an expectation for those who hope to obtain a bachelor's degree. Everything is available with the click of a mouse, and every view creates perceptions—some realistic, some unrealistic. The power of information and technology is driving customer expectations to higher and higher levels.

Higher education customer expectations are also influenced by customer service practices from other industries, a spillover effect of sorts. Hotel chains, online retailers, and automobile repair shops are all focusing on customer service and are training their employees to maximize the customer experience. Business organizations know that their products and services are easily copied, but employees committed to excellent service delivery provide the one remaining differentiator. Admittedly, buying an education is a little different from staying overnight at a hotel or visiting an amusement park. Still, experiences outside of higher education influence the service delivery people expect from higher education. Internal customers are not immune from this spillover effect either, and that is why they, too, have escalating expectations for service delivery.

The Four Customer Types

Despite the technology, the comparisons, and all of the choices, higher education professionals have a few tools left not only to meet but exceed customer expectations. It is possible to turn both your internal and external customers into what Dr. Ken Blanchard has termed *raving fans*—and not just on the football field! Raving fan customers are so impressed with your service that they will literally "write home" about how you exceeded their expectations. The key to creating customers who will rave about your service lies in unlocking the relationship between customer expectations and customer satisfaction.

First, we offer some background on expectations, which are closely related to needs. A need is a natural or self-created requirement. In today's world of technological capability and 24/7 access, we expect all departments, offices, and people (even friends and family members) to meet our needs. Our needs (or perceived needs) relate to convenience, immediacy, accuracy, fulfillment, accomplishment, and even emotional connection. When we expect someone to meet our needs, it is because we cannot obtain something desirable on our own. We need help. If someone helps us meet our needs (by providing a service), that means they have probably met an expectation. If our expectations are not met, even if someone tried to help us, we feel disappointed and upset.

In *Mind over Mind: The Surprising Power of Expectations*, Chris Berdik explains the relationship between trust and expectations. Berdik explains that trust occurs at a cognitive level, producing positive responses in our internal reward systems. When trust is broken, feelings similar to pain may emerge. These deep reactions explain why customers become loyal when their expectations are met but show frustration when they are not met. If your expectations are met by someone else, this triggers a positive response toward the person (or campus office) who met that expectation. This leads to psychological trust. Under normal circumstances, if your expectations are not met, there is no trigger to the internal reward system and, hence, no trust. It is here that Berdik's insight can be used to get beyond "under normal circumstances." By practicing the many attributes of good service delivery that you defined in Chapter 1, customers will still experience a positive response (based on the trust you have established), even if you are not able to meet their expectations immediately.

Satisfaction is also part of the customer service equation, but it must be understood in tandem with expectations. In most situations, we assume that satisfaction is a natural result of meeting expectations. A student goes to an academic advisor for advice on semester course work. The student receives that advice in a friendly, professional manner and thus is satisfied with the advisor's service. If the student goes to the academic advisor but does not feel she was helped, she will be dissatisfied with the service.

Sometimes a service provider meets expectations but fails to generate customer satisfaction. This usually happens when the customer has been carrying the expectation for some time. Time goes by, and the provider still has not met the expectation. Finally, when the service is delivered and the expectation is met, the customer is not satisfied. She has been waiting so long that that she may be angry and upset rather than grateful and satisfied. Perhaps you, as an internal customer, have had the experience of waiting for a budget report from a colleague to determine whether there was enough money to deliver a student leadership program at three different times during the semester. Your colleague has the information but is slow to get you the report and keeps promising it is coming. By the time you receive the budget report, you only have time to organize and deliver two programs, even though the budget would have allowed for three. In this situation, you would not be a satisfied customer.

A final scenario involving satisfaction and expectations is somewhat counterintuitive: creating satisfaction without meeting expectations. Recall that expectations come from our needs. There are two types of needs: conscious and subconscious. We all consciously formulate expectations based on our own needs. We may also develop expectations based on excellent service we have received in the past, so we expect that same excellent service in the future. Conscious expectations are easy for us to articulate because they are things we are thinking about at the moment. They are at the top of our minds. If Erin goes to her academic advisor to set up her schedule for next semester, she consciously expects to come out of the meeting with a defined schedule. After all, she set up the meeting so she could plan her work activities proactively around her course schedule. Unlike conscious needs, subconscious needs lie beneath the surface. They are there, but we are just not aware of them. We have no conscious expectations developed around subconscious needs. Needs that are not urgent may be subconscious just because there are other more immediate needs drawing our attention. A service provider may also bring a subconscious need to the surface. This might be referred to as creating a need. When you find yourself pleasantly surprised or wondering what you ever did without a service, then the person or organization providing the service has done a good job bringing your subconscious needs to the surface and creating satisfaction. Mike may have never thought about whether he would have Internet access at the student union, but he is happy and satisfied when he discovers he can check NCAA tournament basketball scores on his tablet when he sits down to lunch.

The dynamic and sometimes complex interaction between customer expectations and customer satisfaction produces different types of customers and how each views us as service providers. Figure 5.1 profiles the four different customer types based on expectations and satisfaction.

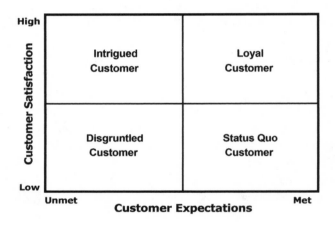

Figure 5.1   Customer Types.

The Loyal Customer

The best type of customer is a loyal customer. The source of a loyal customer's high satisfaction is the service provider's ability to meet the customer's conscious expectations. Loyalty and trust are developed through consistent service delivery that meets and even exceeds expectations. Opportunities to exceed expectations are all around us. No matter where you work on campus, you have a good chance of exceeding customer expectations if you (a) apply the excellent customer service practices from Chapter 1 and (b) make the effort to really know your customers by completing the exercises in Chapters 2 and 3.

Paul works in the print shop at a large institution. He puts excellent customer service principles into action, and he knows his customers well or works to find out more about them. He creates high satisfaction by meeting and exceeding expectations. The usual perception of a university print shop is that it handles regular print job orders from faculty and staff and maybe takes on a couple of extra duties during downtimes. It is never downtime in Paul's office; he and his staff go out of their way to reach out to the campus and surrounding community. The print shop workers not only are knowledgeable about their products, but they also are extremely friendly to students and staff alike. In-house graphic designers work to make brochures, signs, and books match the visions of their customers. The print shop is also a savvy advertiser, letting campus organizations and local businesses know about the shop's variety of services. At an annual open house, the print shop provides tours of its state-of-the-art machinery and distributes samples of different products.

Paul and his staff follow a simple communication process to ensure that they understand every customer's needs and expectations. The team's standard practice is to sit down with the customer and perform a needs assessment. After the assessment, the team provides the customer with a list of options based on the parameters of the original request. The options usually include new suggestions that the customer had not even thought about. The print shop also keeps a record of every project, in case customers make similar requests in the future. The mission of the print shop is to provide a great customer service experience. The staff does an excellent job fulfilling this mission by consciously focusing on customer service. The result: loyal customers who keep coming back.

Loyal customers are repeat customers. Loyal external customers ensure the good reputation of your office and reinforce its value through strong word of mouth. Loyal internal customers ensure your reputation as a valuable colleague and contributor to the campus community. Building a base of loyal internal and external customers is easier than people think, for it is often the small things that a professional does that tap the human satisfaction that comes from meeting or exceeding expectations.

The Status Quo Customer

A common but mistaken assumption is that if you meet the customer's expectations, then satisfaction automatically follows. The problem with this assumption is that it does not distinguish between expectations and satisfaction. They are related but not exactly the same.

Campus offices that have mostly status quo customers do enough to get by—just to meet the expectation—but no more. Measuring service performance based on a minimally acceptable service standard makes it difficult to generate loyal customers. Status quo customers won't complain about your service, but they certainly won't rave about it either. Status quo customers will not generate the word of mouth that is so valuable to any office or individual service provider on campus.

In higher education, there are many instances where an office could just meet the bare minimum and get by. But many professionals go beyond the status quo. Think of the help desk of the IT department that answers questions regarding your institution's learning management system, such as Blackboard or Moodle. Instructors need assistance as they prepare their online courses for the upcoming semester. Students need login or installation help. If the help desk personnel answer questions in a perfunctory manner, customers may still get the help they need, but they may not feel very good about it. In this case, the help desk is providing adequate customer service and doing just enough to meet standards of performance. Students and faculty will become or remain status quo customers.

To transform status quo customers into loyal customers, the help desk can provide additional hints or shortcuts related to the customer's request. This goes above and beyond the original request. One faculty member reported to us his request for help setting up an online final examination, something he had never done before. Initially, the help desk provided the standard telephone support that accompanies such a request. It soon became apparent to the service representative that the professor was uncomfortable putting the exam online. The service representative suggested a face-to-face meeting at the faculty member's office, to walk through the process together. That is service that goes above and beyond. At our own institution, we have received follow-up e-mails and phone calls from the help desk to ensure that a request was solved, or to ask whether IT could provide anything else.

The challenge for any higher education professional or department is that customer satisfaction is a moving target. All those customers who receive great customer service from the IT department now expect continued great service. You set a high bar when you exceed expectations, and it takes effort to maintain that level of service. Once a need is met, it soon becomes an expectation.

The defining feature of a status quo customer, then, is a customer whose expectations were met but whose satisfaction remains low. Satisfaction remains low because the customer was expecting the service you provided and there was no significant memory or meaning created through the service delivery process. Status quo customers do not tell others about your great service, and their return as repeat customers is not guaranteed. They will not complain, but they will not be raving fans either. Status quo customers may be quick to try alternatives and seek new solutions because they feel no loyalty to you.

Everyone expects quick, friendly service wherever they go—that is the baseline of customer service. Everyone expects the librarian to help find journal articles, the writing center to help edit a paper, and the campus police to be available 24/7. We should not assume that a customer will be satisfied just because we met baseline expectations. It takes better-than-average service to transform status quo customers into something more.

The Intrigued Customer

Imagine you had never heard of the movie director Peter Jackson, but you agreed to accompany us to his latest movie. You had no expectations because you did not know anything about Jackson's previous movies (*King Kong, The Lord of the Rings, The Hobbit,* and other films). As we take our seats and the movie progresses, you lose yourself in the movie. You feel emotion as you watch. Two hours seems like ten minutes. Your need for entertainment, escapism, and intrigue is fulfilled. You are happy and satisfied after the movie, even though you entered the theater without any expectations. You even ask us about other movies Jackson has directed, because you are curious to see more of his films. Your experience has left you fully satisfied, even though you had no expectations.

It may seem impossible to create customer satisfaction when the customer has no expectations in the first place. But what if you intrigue the customer by fulfilling a need the customer was not expecting or did not even know he or she had? Remember, needs lie beneath expectations. It is only after customers become conscious of these needs and simultaneously experience the satisfaction of having them met that they develop expectations.

The idea of creating satisfaction by fulfilling a need or intriguing the customer is applicable in any environment, including higher education. Let's take campus dining as an example. On a residential campus, students typically purchase a meal plan. They may not necessarily expect to find anything other than typical college fare served at the dining facility. New students are often surprised at the large selection of foods available. Not only do many campus dining services provide a wide variety of cultural foods, but healthy alternatives and organic choices have become the norm. Nutritional values are prominently displayed, and a student can even attend seminars on healthy eating, sustainability, and recycling. Even though students may be unaware of the many benefits they are going to receive from dining services, they quickly appreciate the value of choice, quality, and nutritional education. Many students become faithful customers of their campus's dining services throughout their college years. These intrigued customers may also bring friends to enjoy a meal or spread the word about healthy and convenient eating. Dining services across the country have done an excellent job of creating nutritional awareness and producing satisfied customers.

Intrigued customers will talk about your services because there is an element of surprise or curiosity. The human propensity to share surprises or talk about unexpected services with others generates positive advertising. But intrigue does not last forever. Initial surprise and curiosity soon develop into expectation. The goal of any campus department or office is to then convert an intrigued customer into a loyal one. With consistent and excellent service, the intrigued customer will soon become a loyal one.

The Disgruntled Customer

Disgruntled customers have unmet expectations and low levels of satisfaction. It is unlikely that any organization could survive for very long with even a small percentage of disgruntled customers. A 2011 marketing study by COLLOQUY, an organization that comprises a collection of resources devoted to the global loyalty marketing industry, found that a person is 26% more likely to spread the word about a bad experience than a good one. COLLOQUY's formidable research arm confirms the long-held belief that unhappy customers are very willing and motivated to tell others they are unhappy. All of this means disgruntled customers can have a disproportionately negative effect on your institution.

Higher education professionals can guard against creating negative perceptions that result in disgruntled customers, even in the face of challenges that strain their service delivery efforts. Budget cuts have placed added responsibilities on almost every position. One person is now doing the same job that used to be done by two or even three people. Betty is an academic advisor at a large, urban community college. When she first started, she was responsible for the students whose last names began with the letters *M* through *P*. Her days were full of advising appointments, but she was able to provide quality, individualized services to her advisees. Recently, the college implemented targeted cutbacks across campus, including a reduction of two employees in the advising office. Betty soon found herself responsible for *M* through *T* students, a significant increase in her student load. Inevitably, the amount of time she was able to spend with each student decreased, and advising has almost come to resemble a factory production line. Betty is frustrated, and students are complaining that they feel like numbers. Betty feels that administration did not use any rationale in deciding where to make cutbacks, so she is upset with her manager and director (disgruntled internal customer) because the advising team received no explanation. Given student reactions to advising services after the cuts, the department is at risk of creating several disgruntled external customers.

Betty's situation is one that higher education professionals at many institutions face. Unpredictable funding is a reality, but staff and managers must work together to find solutions to minimize the negative impact on customers. Betty's managers probably felt bad about the cuts and tried to make their case to upper administration to save the two positions. But when it was clear the cuts were going to happen, Betty's manager and director isolated themselves instead of gathering the team to develop ideas and perhaps define new work processes to minimize the impact. The result has been disgruntled internal and external customers.

Institutional departments and divisions may inadvertently create disgruntled customers. Many services that departments provide are hard for students and the general public to understand. The complex rules and regulations regarding financial aid are one example. Students and parents who are not knowledgeable about financial aid rely on explanations from professionals. Misunderstandings and misperceptions are common in any industry where the customer is heavily dependent on the service provider's advice and knowledge. Effective, simple communication is the service antidote. We have all seen the stereotypical television scene where a doctor uses technical terms to communicate with a patient, leaving the patient even more confused and frustrated. Higher education professionals who avoid technical industry jargon during customer interactions avoid this trap.

A second behavior institutions can monitor is the tendency to adopt a cavalier attitude toward customers when organizations believe they are "the only game in town." In some rural counties, there may be just one postsecondary institution. Providers who believe they have a monopoly tend to ignore customer service, since even disgruntled customers have only one option. Most higher education professionals realize that with online offerings, no institution is a monopoly. Customer service is a must in rural and urban areas, and it is an effective strategy to meet customer needs, maintain satisfaction, and compete with the growing postsecondary options available to students.

The main takeaway from any discussion involving disgruntled customers is that you cannot afford to dismiss them. Disgruntled customers are very predictable in that they want to tell other people about the source of their unhappiness. Disgruntled customers will tell other people about the problems they had on your campus and how you did not meet their expectations. If they can't express their dissatisfaction to another person, they will take it to the Internet. A good dose of excellent customer service will prevent your customers from ever reaching this stage.

Identifying Your Customers by Type

If you take an inventory of your current customers, how would you classify them according to the four customer types? Think about your external and internal customers and then complete the right-hand column of Exercise 11.

EXERCISE 11 Customer Types	
Customer Type	Percent of Total Customer Base
Loyal Customer	
Intrigued Customer	
Status Quo Customer	
Disgruntled Customer	
TOTAL PERCENT	100%

Ideally, you want 100% loyal customers and 0% disgruntled customers, but this is not realistic. It is impossible to have only loyal customers. How does your completed table look? Is there an ideal mix of customer types to strive for? Here are some helpful parameters to set your customer service goals. These parameters are guided by what is commonly known as Pareto's law, or what author Richard Koch calls the 80/20 principle (in his book *The 80/20 Principle*).

- At least 80% of your customers should fall in the loyal category.
- Less than 20% of your customers should be, at any point, intrigued, status quo, or disgruntled.
- Of the 20% who are intrigued, status quo, or disgruntled, 80% should be in the intrigued category, giving you a chance to convert them to loyal customers.
- Of the 20% who are intrigued, status quo, or disgruntled, no more than 15% should be in the status quo category, giving you a chance to convert them to intrigued or loyal customers.
- Of the 20% who are intrigued, status quo, or disgruntled, less than 5% should be in the disgruntled category. This means that for every 100 customers, you should be dealing with no more than one customer who is disgruntled.

Imagine that your department routinely deals with 100 students per week. Of those 100 students, let us assume that ten of them are disgruntled. Ten disgruntled students out of 100 students is a very precarious situation. This can lead to widespread negative publicity and bad word of mouth about your department and institution. Even five disgruntled students may outweigh the positive message that 20 loyal and intrigued customers spread. Disgruntled students will seek out more people to talk to about their perceptions than will loyal or intrigued customers.

It is unavoidable that some of your customers are going to get upset for one reason or another. Your goal is to make sure that those upset customers do not exceed one of every 100 customers. This will give you a good chance to manage that disgruntled customer and figure out the problem. You must help disgruntled customers solve their problems, even if they never come back. It is always better if a disgruntled customer leaves a little less disgruntled, and it may even help you uncover a potential problem with other customers. Once the disgruntled customer's emotional reaction subsides, the individual may actually return at some other time knowing you worked to solve his or her problem.

The percentages you identified in Exercise 11 help you look at your services from a customer perspective. You may find it beneficial to separate your internal and external customers for purposes of Exercise 11. Aim for the ideal of 100% customer satisfaction, knowing that no institution or department has only loyal customers. Also remember that disgruntled customers may become upset with you or your office, not because of something you did but because of another experience somewhere on or off campus. Still, do everything you can to help all of your customers and reach for the ideals that define great customer service.

Customer Expectations Summary

Customer expectations are not static. Changing preferences, needs, wants, and desires drive changing expectations. Internal and external customers also formulate expectations based on their service experiences inside and outside of higher education, and they subconsciously compare your personal service delivery against those experiences. Each customer is unique and carries different expectations about what leads to true satisfaction. The portrait of the four customer types is a tool to help you, as a higher education professional, understand why customers may differ in what they expect and how they come to think about a satisfying customer experience. Creating loyal customers is a matter of common sense: Take the time to understand your customers and assess their needs. Make common sense common practice.

Chapter 5 Takeaways

- Underneath every customer expectation lies a need, which a customer expects a service provider to fulfill.
- A satisfied customer may or may not spread the good word about your service delivery, but an unsatisfied customer will surely share negative perceptions about it.
- There are four customer types: loyal, intrigued, status quo, and disgruntled.
- To create more loyal customers, go back to the basics: Understand your customers (Chapters 2 and 3) and implement excellent service delivery practices (Chapter 1).

6

CREATING A CULTURE OF SERVICE

Every organization has a culture, and higher education professionals live within these cultures. The culture of an organization affects group dynamics, interpersonal relationships, and team performance. Although this chapter is not about department mergers, the influence of culture on organizational and team interaction and performance becomes very apparent when administrators attempt to merge academic or administrative departments. Department mergers and other forms of restructuring are common in higher education, especially during funding declines for public institutions. Directors and vice presidents are often under extreme pressure to find efficiencies and lower costs. In most cases, the effort to merge two or more departments on a campus is an attempt to save administrative costs by combining related functions or those departments that perhaps deliver complementary services to their customers. Some institutions have combined housing and dining while others have merged admissions and international programs or recruitment and orientation departments.

Administrative optimism about the anticipated savings and efficiencies from departmental mergers and restructuring initiatives is often short-lived. The focus on cost savings sometimes means that little attention is paid to the realities of cultural differences across campus functions and departments. The failure to account for human and cultural differences is, according to many of Stanford professor Jeffrey Pfeffer's writings, the reason for the high rate of failure of business mergers. There is little reason to believe the same isn't true with internal mergers in colleges and universities.

An examination of how recruiters and orientation staff do their work demonstrates how different cultures develop around these two professions and may make merging their offices problematic, if they initially are separate departments. Recruiters and orientation staff both connect and communicate with entering or potential freshmen, but the tasks that each performs also mean different practices, values, and ways of doing work have formed in these two professions. A recruiter's tasks include visiting local and regional high schools, meeting with school counselors, and making presentations. The recruiter's job largely takes place off campus and may involve a good deal of travel to persuade potential applicants about the virtues of the recruiter's campus. When recruiters attend on-campus events, they historically have not helped to any great extent with the logistical tasks associated with event management. Instead, they are mostly "front-of-the-house" and represent the institution once the event happens. Orientation staff are often the behind-the-scenes logistical coordinators (scheduling, transportation, dining, housing, etc.) who make large-scale campus events happen. Orientation staff also design programs to acclimate entering freshmen who are already admitted to the institution. Orientation staff keep more traditional business hours and stay on campus. All of these differences add up to different cultures. These differences could lead to merger challenges that end up requiring significant administrative attention. It is not too difficult to see, for example, how orientation staff may feel a bit confused when their new colleagues are rarely in the office and do not contribute to logistical tasks in a newly merged department. Even though orientation staff understand that recruiters have a different function, they will still compare their time in the office with the recruiters' lack of office time, especially when everyone is asked to help with new office duties. The recruiters may feel that expectations to contribute to administrative duties on campus, due to a merger, interfere with their main job responsibilities. These differences can become very pronounced and end up costing more time and money, all because administrators focused only on cost savings and ignored the challenges associated with merging two different cultures.

The recruiter culture is not better or worse than the orientation staff culture; it is just different. Two organizational cultures have developed around these professions. Organizational cultures encompass the way people behave, the way they dress, how they serve customers, and how they accomplish their goals. Other elements of organizational culture include the rules people must follow to do their jobs, the lines of authority outlined in the commonly known organizational or reporting charts, the vocabulary and acronyms people in the field use, and the little "tricks of the trade" that are not written in any manual but are crucial to career success.

The connection between culture and service is sometimes difficult to make, since culture is simply a part of who we are and what we do. Culture is always present but sometimes we are not aware of it, much like the air we breathe. Though there are many aspects to organizational culture, three directly affect service delivery and, therefore, contribute to what we might term a *service culture* in higher education:

1. formal structures, which include reporting charts and the physical layout of the office;
2. the way the work is done, or the work processes; and
3. the deep-rooted, collective values, beliefs, and behaviors of the organization.

Some elements of service culture are easier to change than others, and all of these elements interact in complex ways that influence professional staff and their level of service delivery. Ultimately, the many service successes and challenges we experience are influenced by the service cultures of our campus offices.

The Effects of Formal Structures on Service

The very word *organization* evokes an image of a reporting chart with boxes and arrows showing who reports to whom. Many of these diagrams look like a confusing maze of roads traveling through a very busy city, especially for large community colleges and universities. But reporting charts are important because they spell out the formal relationships between administrators and staff across a campus. These relationships guide internal customer interactions, so they are an important influence on service delivery.

Paula recently assumed duties as the judicial affairs officer on her campus. Paula reports directly to the dean of student affairs, and this is shown on a campus-wide reporting chart. The dean provided Paula with an additional reporting chart when she started her new position that is much more detailed. This reporting chart shows that Paula is at a similar range of pay and responsibility as other directors on campus. The directors are all "dotted lines" to each other, because they must work together, depending on the nature of the student issue at hand. Paula may need to work with the directors of the office of residential life, the university police department, or the fraternity and sorority affairs office. The supplemental reporting chart Paula received simply helps to identify other colleagues she may need to work with as particular issues arise.

A well-constructed reporting chart clarifies who ultimately has decision-making responsibility. This provides consistency for employees, customers, or anyone linked to the organization. An ill-conceived reporting chart can create a lot of confusion. Connie and two colleagues coordinated a major grant, which was housed in a student success center on campus. The center comprised three different departments, all of which were contributing to the grant's success. Thus Connie and her team provided support to all three departments and formally reported to all three department managers. Connie and her two colleagues often found themselves disagreeing on implementation issues and were finding it hard to get along. The question was: Where was the problem? Was Connie's team ineffective? Was it a management problem?

As it turned out, the problem was in the reporting chart. Connie and her team were serving three different managers with equal authority, a recipe for disaster. Two of the managers did not see eye-to-eye on a number of issues. One manager often would tell Connie's two colleagues to do one thing, but then the other manager would tell Connie to do something completely different. Connie and her team were caught in an escalating competition between the two managers, which caused confusion and disagreement. With the dysfunctional reporting structure, the departments began to feel that Connie and her colleagues were not providing good customer service. It did not take a consultant long to point out the problem to the director of the success center. With little knowledge of the division's problems, the consultant looked at the reporting chart and described, to the director's amazement, virtually every ailment that was plaguing the center. This example, from an actual campus office, demonstrates how important reporting relationships are to service delivery. A properly designed reporting chart ensures effective internal communication, which then supports external customer service.

Physical Layout and Distance

The physical layout of a work environment can facilitate or inhibit service delivery. The physical layout of a two-story fire station demonstrates this point. We normally think of a fire station as an orderly, open building that is easy to move through; there are no private, soundproof offices or cubicles. All of the fire trucks are parked on the first floor of the building, and the firefighters eat, rest, and exercise on the second floor. When the alarm sounds, the firefighters quickly get their gear and slide down the pole that connects the second story to the first. Response times are almost immediate, partly because the layout of the fire station is neat and orderly, not cluttered and mazelike.

Many higher education administrative offices have arranged the physical layout of their offices using cubicles whose arrangement resembles a maze. Though many vice presidents and directors have offices, it is not uncommon to find both administrators and professional staff working in cubicles.

Philosophically, cubicles are supposed to connote equality and democracy, and the physical layout of the office reinforces these cultural values. The purpose of cubicles is also to increase interaction and accessibility. From a service perspective, this interaction and accessibility improves communication and, therefore, service delivery to internal and external customers. Accessibility to colleagues also increases information flow and idea exchange.

For many campuses, cubicles in higher education administration offices may represent practical realities more than philosophical ideals. As space across campuses becomes scarce, cubicles become a cost-effective solution to house a growing number of staff who must meet the needs of a growing institution. Ideally, the physical layout of an organization should depend on its function. While student affairs staff may find working in cubicles an acceptable solution (though perhaps not preferred), professors typically have offices with doors. Student affairs staff work in a highly interactive environment, as they constantly interact with internal and external customers. University professors are required to write, and writing requires concentration, quiet, and solitude. For administrative staff, the real influence of physical layout on service delivery remains its influence on internal and external customer interaction. If reporting charts and the office layout contribute to efficient internal communication between and among employees, this will likely improve external customer service as well.

Reporting charts and office layout are both what might be referred to as structural elements of the service culture. These elements can influence interpersonal relationships in subtle ways. Dawn is a graduate student in a higher education program and a graduate assistant in the student involvement office at a local community college. Various student affairs and support services are clustered together in the same building in which Dawn works, which means that most employees work in cubicles. The college president and executive vice president created this clustering to offer students "one-stop" service delivery, meaning that students can go to one convenient location to receive any student-related service.

Dawn's cubicle is next to Ellen's. Ellen is the student involvement coordinator. Dawn and Ellen have gotten to know each other quite well, both professionally and personally. Dawn is well aware of changes or issues that are happening in the office because Ellen often updates her during their regular, brief visits. So when issues arise, Dawn is in the know, which has improved her responsiveness to customers. Compared to the other graduate assistants and student workers in the office, Dawn's last evaluation was glowing, and a large part of that was because she delivers fast, friendly, and reliable external customer service.

Another part of Dawn's excellent performance is attributable to human nature. Dawn benefited from Ellen's firsthand information about issues and problems, and this certainly allowed Dawn to improve her service delivery. People who work in close proximity to each other naturally begin to develop a relationship, which means frequent communication. This was true of Dawn and Ellen, and it is true of countless other coworkers. Most relationships at the office consist of professional and personal components, and the two often become comingled. Social psychologist Elliot Aronson, in his foundational textbook *The Social Animal*, says that we are naturally curious about others, especially when we find something interesting about them or if we find a commonality. We then begin to look favorably on that person.

Dawn and Ellen's increased interaction was the result of the physical layout of their office, which resulted in their close proximity to each other. You should not rush to be relocated next to your manager just because of this example, but it is helpful to understand that physical layout and distance affect relationships and communication within an office environment. This, in turn, influences service delivery.

The effect of physical layout and proximity of service culture is undergoing some change. More and more college and university professionals are completing tasks remotely or delivering services online. A natural by-product of offering, say, online counseling, is changing office dynamics. Higher education professionals communicate and interact in different ways when some services are offered online or colleagues work remotely. Most college employees still travel to work and spend the majority of the day inside a campus building with offices and people, but it will be important to gauge how technology continues to affect the services we offer, how we do our work, and how we interact with each other—all of which are critical pieces of service culture.

Work Processes and Service Delivery

A *work process* is the way work gets done. In some organizational cultures, strict rules govern the work processes; in other cultures, there are no rules. Dan has been the director of the advising center and coordinator of undergraduate advising on a small campus for three years. Dan's staff is very experienced, and though every advisor has processes to follow and boundaries within which to operate, there is also a good deal of freedom in crafting solutions for certain students who come for advising. Dan found in his previous management role that inexperienced advisors follow templates and advising sheets very closely, and they are most comfortable advising students majoring in traditional fields such as psychology or economics. As advisors gain experience, they become more comfortable working with students who are interested in interdisciplinary studies—students who need some degree of customization because their programs do not always follow a set template of courses.

Many things determine whether a work process is rigid or flexible. Flexibility in work processes may be a product of the administrator's management style or even the function of the office. Several offices on campus must follow government regulations and policies, and, therefore, their work processes are well defined and there is little flexibility. If employees stray too far from standard work processes that are designed to adhere to these regulations and policies, legal problems may result. Figure 6.1 shows that the work processes associated with any job or organization can range from strict to flexible. Where a given work process falls on this continuum depends on the nature of the work and, often, the size of the organization. Larger organizations tend to standardize their work processes in an effort to provide consistent customer service.

Figure 6.1 provides some general guidelines for where we might find flexible versus strictly defined work processes, but there may be big differences even within the same office. The HR office on campus covers a range of services, from talent management to benefits. Many aspects of benefits are subject to federal or even state law, so professionals working in benefits probably find very defined work processes. Those who are charged with the progressive-sounding

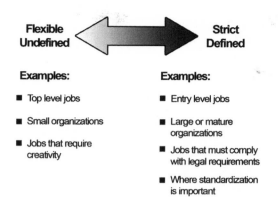

Figure 6.1   The Nature of Work Processes.

"talent management" function must creatively look for solutions to fill the institution's workforce with capable people. Work processes in this area of HR are less defined.

Work processes may differ not just within an office such as HR, but even for one person who has multiple responsibilities within that office. Jean works on a small community college campus in HR, so that means she must wear many hats. One day she may find herself following strict rules when dealing with grievance, complaint, or sexual harassment issues. Jean is also involved in defining the competencies employees need in order to make the organization successful. She has a lot of freedom in this aspect of her job. She conducts assessments and mini focus groups with employees; she designs training; and she often contracts and negotiates with outside vendors to provide training. Because of Jean's different duties, some of her work processes are strict while others are flexible.

No matter where you place your job on Figure 6.1, one type of work process is not necessarily better than another. Higher education professionals work in a range of jobs, from designing student leadership programs to managing faculty, staff, and student records. It is the nature of the job and the talents of the professionals who do those jobs that determine how strict or flexible a work process may or may not be. And people like to do different jobs, so they enjoy delivering different types of services. Student development professionals might enjoy designing programs and presenting them to large groups; institutional researchers might like to analyze campus data and then fashion recommendations for central administrators.

Work Process Design and Customer Service

Work processes include more than just how individual people do their jobs; they also include how the organization does its job. Such work processes are more accurately called internal work processes because they include the internal rules that everyone must follow to do things such as buy computers and pens or arrange for travel. Good internal work processes allow you to be more efficient and productive. What if your manager did not have discretion over minimal spending amounts and had to follow similar procedures for both small and large purchases? This work process might create unnecessary roadblocks for you. It would not make sense to require a supervisor to obtain four levels of upper-management signatures to purchase a $100 piece of software you need to do your job. That is a bad work process. Your institution might require two levels of signatures for any acquisition over $5,000, however, and that may not be a bad idea since this is not a nominal amount of money.

Internal work processes are important for another reason—they directly affect how we provide customer service. Many times it is possible to examine the "design" of a work process and assess whether it is helping or hurting customer service. Technology may help improve customer service and make processes more efficient. We have seen technology used in airports, grocery stores, and banking, all in ways that have improved efficiency and helped people access services 24/7. This is called process innovation.

A good example of how work processes affect service delivery is the *Theater Experience on Campus* explained in Chapter 4. The *Theater Experience on Campus* is identified as a Cycle of Service. A Cycle of Service is a series of events, or moments, that relates to service delivery and thus influences customer satisfaction. One Moment of Truth is called "Ticket office," the time when the customer buys or picks up a ticket from the box office. The traditional process by which customers buy tickets is shown in Figure 6.2.

Figure 6.2 resembles some ticket offices but also represents the work process that most supermarkets use as customers purchase their goods. Most people try their best to choose the shortest line in this situation, but somehow the person in the front of the line always argues about a price or cannot get his credit card to work. It is only then that you realize it would have been better to choose the longer

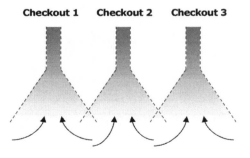

Figure 6.2   Traditional Purchase Process (many lines, many checkouts).

line. In the case of the ticket office, the cashiers are not to blame for the long lines if administrators use the work process shown in Figure 6.2. But customers do want to blame somebody, and the cashier is their immediate point of contact. The traditional work process to help customers is not very empowering if you are the cashier who has to deal with irate customers who have been waiting in a long line.

Banks used to have the traditional checkout problem illustrated in Figure 6.2, but people complained because they were waiting in line for too long. Like the ticket office dilemma, even if you chose the shortest line when you walked in, you often waited the longest because invariably there was some problem with the customer ahead of you. Customers were not satisfied with the service they received at the bank, so they would complain to the tellers. The tellers would be as polite as possible, but by 2:30 p.m., after hearing one person after another complain about the wait, the weather, and whatever else happened to be going wrong, the poor tellers were ready to explode. The entire situation meant customers felt like they were receiving poor service.

Creative Work Process Design

Many years ago, the work process by which banks served their customers was changed in a way that improved service and eased the burden on the tellers. Designers and researchers figured out that the process by which the banks were serving customers could be altered to reduce the average customer's waiting time. Instead of having separate lines and making the customer choose one, a single-file line would reduce each person's waiting time. This new work process meant that no customer had to choose a line. Everyone was in the same line, and then the next available teller helped the next person in the single-file line. Today, lines inside banks look like Figure 6.3 and are much more efficient. The

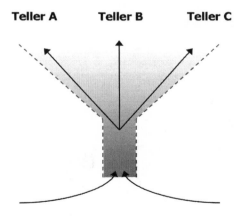

Figure 6.3 A New Work Process (single line, many tellers).

customer's Moment of Truth at the ticket office on campus would minimize complaints if campus administrators designed the work process like Figure 6.3. The same would be true for lines where students are ordering transcripts or receiving any other type of service on campus.

Work processes influence customer service delivery and customer satisfaction. Sometimes research, common sense, or new ideas can help streamline work processes and contribute to process innovation. Process innovation, in turn, helps people do their work more effectively and deliver more efficient service.

Clever redesigns, like the one shown in Figure 6.3, do not require technology yet can markedly improve service delivery. But just as technology influences physical distance and interaction, it might also help institutions improve work processes. A good example of this is the old procedures that employees had to follow when seeking permission to take a trip, purchase office supplies, or advertise for a staff position. Many higher education professionals remember when such requests had to go through the internal campus mail system for signature approvals. Some organizations still use internal mail for practically every form that needs to be signed, but it takes weeks to get a simple travel request approved or reimbursed. The problem is usually that three to four people have to approve the request. The paperwork often gets stuck in someone's in-box because the recipient forgot about it or perhaps was traveling or on vacation. Eventually, people start blaming one another for not getting requests approved in a timely manner. The real problem is that the organization has not invested in automating the approval process.

If you have ever worked in an office where the approval process for most requests is computerized, you know that employees are more efficient because their requests are approved or rejected quickly. Either way, they have an answer and can act accordingly. In technology-based approval systems, those administrators who grant approval get an e-mail that asks for action every time they log onto the system, and the system can point to the exact person who has to give an answer to the request but has not yet provided one. That is an efficient work process.

Work Process Assessment

An ineffective work process can cause stress, burnout, and misunderstandings—all of which can have a negative effect on internal and external customer service. When people are busy blaming each other for late paperwork, late orders, or irate customers, the result is energy spent arguing and finger-pointing, not better service. Well-designed internal work processes that make appropriate use of technology improve service delivery. Are your organizational or individual work processes facilitating or inhibiting your service delivery? Answer the following questions to find out. If you are working with a team, have your team members answer the questions independently before comparing answers.

Work Process Assessment
1. Do the work processes in your office help you do your job more effectively?
2. Does your job require you to follow strict rules and procedures, or do you need flexibility to individualize service delivery to your customers?
3. Have those recurring processes that can be improved by technology been automated or standardized?

If you answered *yes* to the first question, the work processes in your office environment are contributing to effective service delivery. These work processes may be standardized or flexible, automated or manual, but they facilitate your work at this time. If you hesitated to answer yes, or if you answered no, then the last two questions may help you determine whether the problem is (a) a mismatch between the work processes and the type of work you do, or (b) a failure to use technology to automate those processes that should be standardized. If, for instance, your manager insists on consistent and standard results from everyone on the team, but there are no rules or procedures in place, results will be inconsistent, and so will service delivery.

Work processes are part of organizational culture because they define how people work and how an organization serves its customers. If your work processes are appropriate for the tasks you are trying to complete, you have a tool to do your job well and deliver excellent service. If there are problems with your work processes or the organization's internal work processes, you must remember that the people who improve processes do not have to be scientists, engineers, or highly paid consultants. You are often in the best position to improve the work processes that, in turn, will improve service delivery. You know your job best.

Values and Beliefs

People automatically associate reporting charts and work processes with organizational culture, but like the tip of a gigantic iceberg, much lies beneath the surface. The collective values and beliefs of an organization are elements of service culture that often lie beneath the surface. Values and beliefs explain why reporting charts and work processes look the way they do. Edgar Schein, in his classic book *Organizational Culture and Leadership*, teaches that values and beliefs in any organization are predicated on assumptions that, over time, operate at the subconscious level.

Values and beliefs do not have to remain unspoken or subconscious. The more that management and staff are conscious of service culture values, the more focus and attention will be directed to service delivery. The problem with subconscious values and beliefs is that people do not share an explicit understanding of those values and beliefs. This leads to a lot of assumptions and guessing about values, beliefs, and even the purpose of the organization. Leaders may feel that their mission and vision statements reflect organizational values and beliefs, but this is usually a warning sign that employees and customers would probably give different answers to the questions, "What does this department value?" or "What are its beliefs?" It seems reasonable that people would give different answers to these questions if they read a mission statement and then are asked to extract values and beliefs based on their personal interpretations of that statement. While mission statements should reflect values and beliefs, it is best if those values and beliefs are explicitly stated, documented, and even posted.

A *value* is an important and sustained attitude or feeling about the worth we attach to something. A *belief* is how we go about experiencing, or living, that value. If you value "hard work," then you may believe that it is important to work at least ten hours a day to live that value. Ideally, values drive beliefs. Table 6.1 gives an example of some values and beliefs of a financial aid office we have worked with.

While it may seem obvious that a financial aid office should place high value on access and affordability, the values and beliefs of this office are explicit—so there is no mistaking what management and staff value. A common set of values also serves another function: It helps to remind everyone of the purpose of his or her job. A financial aid administrator who internalizes the importance of access to higher education is much more likely to enjoy her job and do a much

TABLE 6.1 Values and Beliefs of Campus Financial Aid Office	
Values	**Beliefs**
Access	Proper financial aid packages ensure that all capable and motivated students have access to higher education.
Affordability (of college)	Proper financial aid packages mean that a college education becomes affordable to all capable and motivated students.
Student-Centeredness	Our office provides excellent service to any and every student who calls, e-mails, or visits.
Professionalism	We treat each other with respect and dignity, every day and all the time.

better job than a person who just shows up for a paycheck. The values provide a reason to do the job. The financial aid administrator who takes the department's values seriously is also very likely to customize aid packages carefully and efficiently (beliefs) for students to ensure access and maximize affordability.

The power of values and beliefs can even work across organizations, as together they create a shared service culture because of the strength of their convictions. The University of Texas at El Paso (UTEP) and El Paso Community College (EPCC) have formed a collaborative partnership that demonstrates how a service culture develops around common values and beliefs. In this case, two distinct institutions create one powerful service culture. UTEP and EPCC are both deeply committed to equity and student success, particularly for Latinos. Both of these campuses are located on the Mexican border, and years ago they began to work in partnership because of their common values and interests.

Their commitment to equity and success started at the top: The presidents of both institutions publicly conveyed to their faculty and staff that they were in the business of partnering together to increase degree completion and close attainment gaps. This meant that both institutions had to make adjustments so that transfer and articulation agreements would actually result in meaningful student progress. It meant that provosts, directors, and mid-level managers had to work together on committees. The conviction ran through the faculty ranks as well. Faculty from both institutions created discipline-specific councils to define optimal student pathways and address issues of common academic interest, such as common core standards.

The commitment to equity and success at UTEP and EPCC makes their collaboration a national model. Their combined service culture puts students first. Their focus on student success for Latino students is so strong that formal and informal collaborations are continually emerging between the institutions. Advisors from UTEP spend time at EPCC, and advisors from EPCC also spend time at UTEP. A group comprising advisors and counselors for both campuses meets at least twice a year to discuss issues, challenges, practices, and other business related to their collaborative goals. Relationships have formed at the interpersonal level as well. It would not be uncommon for a director of student success at EPCC to call on the dean of entering student programs at UTEP because she views the dean as a resource and colleague.

The collaboration between UTEP and EPCC is not perfect—new challenges arise: a key staff member may leave for another opportunity or a new program doesn't work out quite as planned. It is the shared values, however, that are the foundation of the service culture. The UTEP-EPCC partnership does demonstrate the power of values and how those values create and drive a service-driven culture.

Answer the questions in Exercise 12 to see how familiar you are with the values and beliefs of your department or office.

EXERCISE 12
Values and Beliefs of Your Department

1. List two values that are central to your department/division:

   a. _____

   b. _____

2. List one belief that is central to your department/division:

   a. _____

3. Overall, I believe that employees and managers in my organization live the values and practice the beliefs that are important to us.

   a. Agree

   b. Somewhat agree

   c. Disagree

The first two questions ask you to describe two values and one belief—these should be central to the purpose of your department or division. If you had trouble answering these questions, you are not alone. In many organizations, including higher education institutions, it is assumed that employees and managers know the values and beliefs that define the culture.

If you had no problem answering the first two questions, your institution probably does a good job of articulating its mission and vision and the values and beliefs that support the mission and vision. The last question has to do with practicing the ideals of the organization. Most of us want to work for an organization that lives its values and beliefs, not one that just writes them down but then accepts or even encourages actions and activities that contradict these ideals. If you do not believe that your institution lives its values and beliefs, you have probably experienced motivational problems. Sometimes people in your department do great work, and yet you still had trouble answering questions 1 and 2. In such cases, the team is working hard to deliver excellent service because they have a good idea of purpose but maybe just can't define it.

Additional Pieces of the Service Culture Puzzle

Reporting structures, work processes, values, and beliefs are all pieces of any service culture. And there are more. Service culture also includes the way people within a certain culture speak (language); the way they dress; and the habits, customs, or activities that are part of their group. Finally, service culture includes what is referred to as *climate*. The climate of an organization is the general attitude employees have about their work environment.

Language and Dress

Language illustrates how department cultures vary even within the same institution. A residence assistant in housing might casually ask a colleague if she would like to go to the "DC" to eat, but if the colleague is not from housing, she may not know that the *DC* stands for the *dining complex*. Campus IT departments are famous for using acronyms to describe projects, systems, service requests, and even their own organizations. In general, IT professionals are also a little less formal in conversation than, say, an agent who answers questions for the IRS. If you call the IRS, the person who answers the telephone will refer to you by a formal title, using *Mr.* or *Ms.*, saying something like, "This is Mr. Lee, how may I help you, Ms. Patterson?" Every institution, department, and even group adopts its own language. Language contributes to a strong service culture as long as everyone (including internal and external customers) understands the language.

Dress, like language, is an outward sign of culture. Like language, dress varies across campus offices and departments. It is not uncommon for employees who work in student activities to dress casually. Your coworkers would probably look at you strangely if you arrived for your shift at the recreation center wearing a tie instead of the standard khakis and polo shirt. On the other hand, institutional researchers who meet regularly with central administrators dress business casual or business formal.

Routines, Customs, and Activities

While language and dress are immediately observable elements of a service culture, routines and customs are the behind-the-scenes, internal workings that enable an organization to deliver its services. Routines, customs, and activities define the daily or weekly life of the office. In some departments, it is customary to have parties and get-togethers for even the smallest occasion. People work and play together through shared activities. An example of a routine activity is weekly staff meetings at 9:00 on Monday mornings. The purpose of the meeting is to debrief challenges, recognize small wins, and review the week ahead. This may be a routine meeting in your organization, and everyone knows it is part of the service culture. Some managers have individual monthly check-in meetings—of not more than ten or 15 minutes—with each employee. Other routines, customs, or activities within your organization may include circulating reports, highlighting accomplishments, or conducting monthly brainstorming sessions to streamline processes or improve service.

Organizational Climate

Organizational climate, the final element we include in our review of service culture, is the way people feel about working in their organization, their general attitude about their work environment. It also encompasses whether employees feel the organization is living the values and beliefs it professes to practice. Organizational climate is, therefore, a gauge of the health of the organization. Employee perceptions about the climate are also shaped by employee-manager relationships, coworker relationships, whether people feel processes facilitate or inhibit their work tasks, and individual perceptions of whether their values and beliefs are aligned with the organization's values and beliefs. A quick assessment of organizational climate includes an assessment of all the service culture elements we have covered, plus relational aspects of the workplace. Exercise 13 will give you a sense of climate in your organization. To get an accurate assessment of the climate in your organization, each team member should take the assessment, with items for each question averaged across all team members, including managers.

A neutral climate score might indicate high scores in some areas (e.g., align with the values and beliefs of your organization) but low scores in others (e.g., bad reporting chart or inefficient work processes). So the high and low items average out. A neutral score might also be the result of average scores across the board on all assessment items. You may have discovered that you are neither overly enthusiastic nor particularly down on your work environment. Perhaps you predicted that your coworkers' results would also produce a neutral climate score. An employee whose results indicate a neutral score is what management gurus might label an employee with medium engagement. Employees with a medium level of engagement usually get the job done or do what needs to be done—but not much more. This type of employee won't volunteer for committee work or assignments that the person perceives to fall outside of his or her job duties.

If your score on the Climate Survey was 18 or lower, then this is a real warning sign. Employees who feel they are working in a negative climate find it very difficult to deliver excellent service to external customers. Nine times out of ten, the cause of a negative climate is traceable to dysfunctional relationships. Marcus Buckingham, author of *First Break All the Rules*, has found that employees don't leave their organizations, they leave their managers. This is not to say that the source of the dysfunctional relationship lies only with the manager, but the strained relationship is at the root of the problem. The source of negative climates may include or go beyond negative relationships. People may perceive a negative climate because other cultural elements like work processes and reporting structures do not enable good service delivery but prevent it.

The Climate Survey is just a gauge. Your scores for each item can help point you in the direction of where you resonate with your organization and

EXERCISE 13 Climate Survey					
Answer the questions with respect to your group or organization, using the following scale. 1 = Strongly Disagree 2 = Disagree 3 = Neutral 4 = Agree 5 = Strongly Agree					
	1	2	3	4	5
1. I understand the values and beliefs of my organization.					
2. The values and beliefs of my organization are aligned with my professional values and beliefs.					
3. Work processes in my organization make it easier for me to do my job.					
4. Managers and employees consistently look for new and better ways to deliver service to our customers.					
5. I relate well to my immediate manager.					
6. I have positive working relationships with my coworkers.					
7. The reporting structure in my office facilitates interaction among employees.					
8. Employees and managers have a positive service attitude.					

Instructions for Scoring:
- Add up your score for the assessment by adding all individual item scores.
- Your score should be between 8 and 40.
- If your score is between 30 and 40, you have described a **Positive** organizational climate.
- If your score is between 19 and 29, you have described a **Neutral** organizational climate.
- If your score is between 8 and 18, you have described a **Negative** organizational climate.

If you scored the assessment somewhere between 30 and 40, you are happy in your job, feel productive, and value the relationships you have with coworkers and management. The satisfaction you feel likely translates into excellent service delivery, to both internal and external customers.

where there may be some misalignment. Most powerful, however, is for every employee and manager to take a climate survey periodically and look at the combined results. This gives a more accurate picture of the climate than any one person's survey result.

Creating a Culture of Service Summary

Every service culture comprises people who, in the best case, work together to live certain values and beliefs. We have seen that reporting charts, work processes, and even the manner in which people speak and behave are all reflections of culture. In campus environments, different people prefer different cultural environments. One person may enjoy developing student programs where he has the freedom and flexibility to create what he thinks might be useful, while another person prefers judicial affairs where she can interpret existing rules and policies and apply those to student conduct issues that arise during the semester.

The secret to delivering enthusiastic service—no matter where you work on campus—rests largely in finding a culture that is a fit for you. If your values and beliefs align with the values and beliefs of your institution and campus office, then your commitment to service delivery will follow. We all search for friends, clubs, organizations, neighborhoods, and churches that hold values and beliefs that we can embrace, and we should do the same in our professional lives.

Chapter 6 Takeaways

- Service culture defines many things about a formal group of people: who they are, what they do, how they do things, and why they do what they do.
- The many pieces of service culture, from reporting charts to work processes and values and beliefs, influence service delivery.
- Organizational climate is an indicator of service climate.
- Higher education professionals whose values and beliefs align with the values and beliefs of their organizations have a greater chance of delivering consistent and ongoing service excellence.

MANAGERIAL INFLUENCE ON SERVICE DELIVERY

In the 1990s it became popular to compare managers to leaders. Leaders were associated with setting the sail: the big picture thinkers who conjured up a vision and then inspired employees to follow along. Leaders do the right thing, managers do things right, we were told. Managers take care of the small operational details while leaders spend their days formulating high-level strategies. Leaders do not spend their time resolving internal disagreements (that is the manager's job) because they are too busy positioning the institution.

While there is some value in distinguishing between managers and leaders, any higher education administrator who has formal responsibility for others, at any level, will find the distinction more theoretical than real. Both central administrators and department managers inspire people, but they also manage relationships, conflicts, and customer problems. Vice presidents and supervisors puzzle over work processes and how to streamline them to improve customer service. The ideal of spending one's day defining strategic direction and organizational goals at a departmental, divisional, or institutional level is often interrupted by the imperatives of crises and emergencies at the operational level.

These are the realities of institutional life, but it is also best not to ignore differences among administrators with different levels of managerial responsibility. Administrators and managers working at different levels of the institution certainly apportion their time differently, and their decisions affect a larger or smaller number of people, depending on their span of control. No one would argue that a community college president and department chair for mathematics have the same responsibilities, or that a senior student affairs officer (SSAO) at a large university and a director of academic advising in a college of business should have the same focus. Yet all of these positions require actions traditionally associated with management and leadership at different points and times. The director of academic advising may need to inspire his team or define new goals based on changes happening on campus. He also has the daily responsibilities of interacting with the team, assessing work processes, mediating employee conflicts, or even pitching in to help with an external customer service problem. The SSAO may need to inspire her team as well, it is just that her team comprises managers and supervisors instead of early career professionals. But even at the SSAO level, traditional duties associated with management, like mediating interpersonal conflicts between direct reports, is still a reality of the job. Any SSAO who has been on the job long enough will surely recall disagreements between managers and supervisors that required the SSAO's direct intervention. The interplay between managerial and leadership responsibilities is dynamic and very real for higher education administrators at all levels of the institution.

For purposes of this chapter and ease of communication, we use the term *manager* to refer to any administrator who has formal responsibility for a team of people, within a functional area of the institution. We assume throughout this chapter that managers at all levels engage in both leadership and managerial duties, and we do not delve into the debate over what activities constitute one or the other. The central aim of the chapter is to examine the influence that managers have on customer service delivery.

Managers hold a special place in our institutions, as their jobs put them squarely in the business of service delivery. A manager's purpose is to help a team of professionals to do their jobs. The manager sets the tone and facilitates the team's work by reinforcing, building, or changing the elements of the culture of the group. Most important to service delivery, the manager directly influences internal customer service delivery through interacting with the team and each individual employee. The manager's own interaction and behavior with the team (commonly referred to as management style) influences the quality of service the team delivers. Managers also form perceptions and expectations of each and every employee they manage, and this, too, influences internal and external customer service delivery.

If you are a professional without managerial responsibilities, this chapter will provide insight into the relationship you have with your immediate manager and, therefore, will uncover how that interaction influences your internal or external customer service delivery. You will also gain general insight into management behavior and, perhaps, learn how to manage your manager. If you are a manager in higher education, this chapter will reveal a little about your own tendencies and management behaviors and how they influence the team you serve.

Management Style and Customer Service

Alan's first job after completing his master's degree was working in a progressive new position in the division of student affairs as a professional development coordinator. His responsibilities included serving on various committees related to strategic planning, budgeting, and personnel issues; providing research and assessment for marketing, communications, and professional development for division staff; and contributing to program evaluation and student learning outcomes initiatives. The position was broad but also would give Alan exposure to various aspects of student affairs.

Alan's first director, Betty, was very businesslike and always got straight to the point. All of Alan's coworkers warned him that Betty did not like to hear about anyone's personal life because she thought people would eventually use that information as an excuse for arriving late to work or missing a day. Many of Alan's coworkers had difficulty working for Betty, and the group seemed to have some morale problems. Staff quietly complained that Betty would do better in a corporate culture environment than on a university campus. People got things done, to be sure, but everyone seemed afraid to make mistakes or offer suggestions. Alan was very productive during his first year on the job; he put in long hours and focused on his tasks. Betty was recruited to another institution with higher pay and more visibility because she ran such a "well-oiled" machine that produced results.

Marv replaced Betty as the group's director. He called a staff meeting and said that his first goal was to sit down with each person to discuss ideas, concerns, and perceptions about the group and the work they were doing. Marv followed through with his goal, and because of his ongoing efforts to build relationships and include people in decisions, he became well liked by his employees. After two years under Marv's management, however, Alan found that his group's overall performance and reputation had declined, and there was a sense that the entire group was disorganized.

Reflecting on his experience, Alan discovered that his work was directly influenced by the different management styles of his two directors over the course of his three years. Under Betty, Alan felt pressured and sometimes upset. At the same time, he would look back on his monthly goals and see how productive he had been. He always felt like he delivered top-notch service to his colleagues, and he never went to a committee meeting without feeling fully prepared. Alan did witness the departure of a few valuable staff members who left because of Betty and her inability to connect with employees. Betty's approach even had an effect on how staff treated one another. Under Marv, Alan sensed a strong kinship within the team, and he felt he could go straight to his director with any concern. The social aspect of the job made work fun. But Alan's productivity and confidence also suffered under Marv. Alan did not have to push himself to accomplish work-related goals, and he sometimes found himself attending strategic planning meetings without having done that little extra that he was known for when Betty was his director. Marv did not push him either, and there were no periodic checks to keep Alan on his toes.

Some managers have the "soft skills" that help them relate to employees, while others focus on tasks and results. Both types of managers may bring out the best in their staffs and, as a result, improve internal and external customer service. Alan experienced the extremes with Betty and Marv, and internal and external customer service delivery had its strengths and weaknesses under each—but neither manager seemed well-balanced.

Managers have different management styles, which means they have different ways of communicating and accomplishing their objectives. Managers affect how employees feel about their jobs and how they go about their work. It is just as important for a staff member to know about management styles as it is for a manager. Like Alan, it may be easy for you to slip in some areas of service delivery and job performance based on your relationship with your manager. If you are a manager, a review of management styles will remind you of how managers influence their teams' internal and external customer service.

Two Management Styles

Alan's experience is not unusual. Managers who are not personable with their employees often experience communication problems with them. On the other hand, it is not uncommon for such managers to produce excellent bottom-line results, at least in the short run, much like Alan's first manager, Betty. Managers like Marv are popular with employees but sometimes criticized for not making the "tough decisions" because they are afraid to hurt anyone's feelings. Not all managers fall at one of these two extremes; most fall somewhere between Betty and Marv.

As early as 1964, Robert Blake and Jane Mouton, in their popular Managerial Grid tool, laid the foundation for describing managers like Marv and Betty. Blake and Mouton describe several different management styles along two dimensions: Concern for People and Concern for Results. Their work built on earlier research at the University of Michigan that identified managers with an employee orientation and those with a production orientation. Blake and Mouton would continue to update and revise their Managerial Grid over the next 20 years, and it has remained a useful model to this day. The basic dimensions of the Managerial Grid continue to help employees and managers understand their interactions. We describe the manager who has high concern for results as a *task-centered* manager, and the manager who has high concern for people and relationships as *people-centered*.

A task-centered manager is concerned about results and focuses on policies, rules, work processes, and getting the job done. Results come about because of structure and the emphasis on tasks. The approach such a manager takes to something like committee work is to focus on each person's tasks and timelines. At the extreme, this manager does not focus on managing the relationships between employees who are on a committee unless these relationships are somehow related to getting the job done. A manager at the opposite extreme is the people-centered manager, one who solicits employee input and pays attention to group dynamics. This type of manager is able to motivate people and manage relationships between and among team members. The people-centered manager would probably push for an initial networking lunch or other social gathering prior to the start of major committee work.

A task-centered manager can exhibit characteristics of a people-centered manager, and a people-centered manager can exhibit characteristics of a task-centered manager. Alan's managers represented two extremes, but *most* managers have characteristics of both styles. *Most* situations call for characteristics of both types of management, but there are times when one style is more effective than the other. A task-centered approach might be valuable if there is a pressing deadline, but a people-centered approach might be more appropriate when trying to mollify an angry external customer.

Exercise 14 will help you identify your manager's management style. If you are a manager, director, or even vice president, answer the questions with

EXERCISE 14 Pulse Assessment: Management Style					
Answer the following questions based on your first reaction, placing only one checkmark for each question under the number that best describes your response. Use the following scale: 1 = Strongly Disagree 2 = Disagree 3 = Neutral 4 = Agree 5 = Strongly Agree					
My Manager...	1	2	3	4	5
1. Knows employees (direct reports) on a personal basis					
2. Is very businesslike					
3. Is easily persuaded by vocal employees					
4. Is career-driven and expects the same of everyone else					
5. Is well-liked by employees					
6. Is not afraid to make tough choices					
7. Tries to keep employees informed of changes and new decisions					
8. Is organized and pushes the group to work hard					
Instructions for Scoring: Add up scores for items 1, 3, 5, and 7: Total = _____ Add up scores for items 2, 4, 6, and 8: Total = _____ • If the scores for items 1, 3, 5, and 7 fall between 10 and 20, your manager exhibits characteristics consistent with a people-centered leadership style. • If the scores for items 2, 4, 6, and 8 fall between 10 and 20, your manager exhibits characteristics consistent with a task-centered leadership style.					

respect to the administrator who is your direct manager. In the case of a vice president, this may be a provost or a president. Like supervisors and department managers, provosts and presidents have specific management styles that influence their teams' dynamics and how individuals do their jobs.

Exercise 14 is called a *pulse assessment* because it provides a quick, general indicator of your perceptions of your manager's management style. Problems between you and your manager are more likely to surface if you ranked your manager very high for one style but very low for the other. In other words, the more extreme the scores for your manager, the more likely it is that you have had similar experiences as Alan's with Betty and then Marv.

You can manage your manager by learning about the common strengths and weaknesses associated with the two management styles. If you improve your ability to work with your manager, that will translate into enhanced communication and interaction within your group. This, in turn, means more effective internal and external customer service delivery.

The Task-Centered Manager

Most managers sought their positions because they believe their ideas can help the institution and the division or department they serve. Managers usually come into their position with goals. The differences between task-centered and people-centered managers mean that different managers will try to reach the same goal in different ways. Task-centered managers are serious, achievement-oriented, and driven by accomplishment. They focus on tasks and activities, and they expect much of their employees. Task-centered managers are not afraid of a challenge, but they may have little tolerance for mistakes and lack the social finesse to solve interpersonal conflicts. These managers invest a great amount of time at work and, to a great extent, define themselves by their jobs. It is difficult for them to take criticism or accept ideas different from their own.

There are some things that you can do to build a productive relationship with a task-centered manager. First, remember that this manager is goal-oriented and focused on specific objectives. Look at and make sure you understand the manager's goals and objectives for the group and those that she has set for you. Ask your manager for clarification, if necessary, but do not personalize terse or blunt responses. A task-oriented manager who seems exasperated at having to reiterate goals, objectives, or tasks actually respects the employee who musters the courage to ask for that clarification.

Employees can become upset because a task-centered manager may neglect to address staff concerns or input, especially during times of change. Many task-centered managers announce changes and expect employees to start implementing them. If you lack the resources, time, or training to contribute to the change, you must tell your manager what you need to be successful. A task-centered manager is likely to assume that you have what you need to get the job done unless you speak up. The risk of not asking for needed resources or help is that you may perceive the demands of your job as unreasonable and come to resent your manager. Much like asking for clarification on some particular objective, it takes a certain level of assertiveness to make a request or voice a concern about a change your task-oriented manager has set before you. The task-oriented manager's response may not be the most eloquent, but if she is truly focused on moving the group forward, you will find that initiating the discussion benefits everyone in the end.

The People-Centered Manager

People-centered managers, like Alan's manager Marv, engender trust because they take the time to talk to people. People-centered managers encourage new ideas and are not threatened by employee input. The uncertainty of this approach is that participative decision making may be perceived as a strength or weakness. On the positive side, staff likes to provide feedback and input. Then, when decisions are made, everyone feels good about the decision. On the other hand, we expect our managers to be decisive and not go back and forth because of ten employees who all have different opinions. We want quick results, and most people lack the patience required for true consensus to emerge. A people-centered manager who encourages participation may be perceived as indecisive or weak when he listens to the arguments for and against a particular issue.

Whatever the perceived strengths and weaknesses of a people-centered manager, you should take the opportunity to build a productive work relationship with this type of manager. Team meetings and one-on-one conversations provide forums to convey feedback, express concerns, and make requests that can ultimately help service delivery.

Before Jean was hired as a policy analyst in the chancellor's office for the university and community college system in her state, she worked with a group of six people in a state government personnel office. Jean's manager, Tony, was very people-centered. During challenging times Tony ensured that blame was not passed from person to person, but he could sense a growing frustration among and between staff. Jean thought that there were problems with the way the group was processing its work and these were causing miscommunication, but she couldn't put her finger on it. Tony pressed Jean and the rest of the team for additional suggestions. The team found a consultant who could help the group "map" its processes and define more clearly tasks, customers, deliverables, and timetables. Tony agreed to hire the consultant based on the team's consensus, and over a two-month period, the team identified bottlenecks in its work processes and improved its internal customer service delivery. Tony listened to his people, and Jean and the team provided specific suggestions. Tony's people-centered approach helped solve what turned out to be some fairly technical problems in the group's work processes.

People-oriented managers do not ignore tasks; it is just that they are good at building relationships and they initially tend to talk to people rather than to dissect tasks. Conversely, most task-centered managers do not completely ignore the human side of institutional life, but they are good at structuring work so they tend to emphasize tasks first rather than people. Most managers have a combination of task-centered and people-centered qualities. Your ability to work effectively with any manager on your campus will improve if you have some sense of the different attributes associated with the people-centered and task-centered management styles. A manager's unique combination of styles influences service delivery for the entire team, since it is the manager who by design is the central facilitator for the team. But the manager's special role in the organization means that there are other ways these individuals influence employee service delivery, namely through the expectations they develop about those whom they manage.

Management Expectations and Service Delivery

A more subtle form of management-employee interaction that influences employee productivity and service delivery is unspoken: management expectations of individual staff members. Just as adults form expectations of children—and children are influenced by those expectations—adults form expectations of other adults. We naturally form expectations about others based on appearances, perceptions, interactions, past performance, and many other things. It follows, then, that managers automatically and naturally form expectations about those they manage.

The expectations your manager has of you influence your interaction with others, how you perform your job, and the service you deliver. Many people have no problem believing that a teacher's expectations influence a student's school performance, but they have trouble believing that their manager's expectations influence their work performance. Social psychologist Elliot Aronson, in his foundational book, *The Social Animal*, indicates that one adult's expectations (sender) of another adult (receiver) influence how the receiver feels and acts. Perceptions and assumptions develop into implicit and explicit expectations.

Since most managers manage multiple employees, they develop different expectations and begin to categorize employees based on those expectations. Most of us shudder at the idea of being categorized, because that begins to sound like someone is stereotyping us. But all of us naturally categorize objects, ideas, and even people to make sense of the world. That is how our brain works. It's important to be aware of one's categorizations but not be bound by them.

Given this background, it is hard to blame a manager for naturally developing expectations and categorizations of, say, performance of the employees she manages. One reason managers formulate expectations of their employees is to help them match responsibilities with employees. Suppose an emergency situation arises that requires someone to complete an unexpected task quickly. The manager must ask herself a series of questions: Whom can I trust? Who can get this done in a hurry? Who will put forth the necessary effort to complete this ill-defined task?

Early on in our academic experiences, many of us developed expectations of our classmates based on our perceptions of their potential and actual performance (the grades they received). Think back to when you were in high school. There was the naturally smart girl who got good grades. You just thought she was smart based on how she talked, her confidence in class, maybe even because of unconscious perceptions you formed based on her parents' occupations. Everything added up to a seemingly foregone conclusion: Everyone knew since ninth grade that this girl was going to be the valedictorian—and she was. Then there was the student who was very gifted but a bit lazy. This was the easy-going guy who could have gotten better grades but never fully used his natural ability. Teachers just couldn't figure out how to motivate him. Other students had to work hard because things did not come easily to them, but they never gave up. Their efforts resulted in A and B grades. Finally, some students just didn't seem to care about school, and they had the poor grades to prove it. They gave no indication of wanting to try, rarely said anything, or always said something disruptive.

If you noticed these different "types" of students in the classroom, you can be sure your teacher did, too. Part of the reason the smart girl did so well and the lazy student did so poorly was because of the teacher's (and classmates') expectations of them. Expectations influence performance. A student's performance certainly depends on individual ability and effort, but if a teacher expects that a student will do well, that student stands a good chance of doing well. If a teacher expects that a student will do poorly, there is a good chance that student is going to perform poorly. Expectations are communicated in direct and indirect ways. This concept of performing to expectations is referred to as a self-fulfilling prophecy, or the Pygmalion effect.

Like teachers and classmates, managers also form expectations. A manager's categorization of an employee is based on the employee's performance and potential. Managers develop performance expectations based on past results or on perceptions they have formed about the employee. Managers develop perceptions about an employee's potential based on these same things. Perceptions develop based on interactions, beliefs about job fit, and a hundred other things. The categorizations managers develop occur in higher education and every other type of organization. No organization is immune. Figure 7.1, the Management Assessment Grid, shows how managers assess employees, based

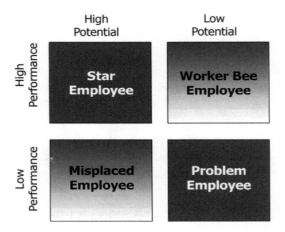

Figure 7.1   Management Assessment Grid.

on the expectations they formulate from the time of hire to their present-day interactions and experiences with the employee.

According to the Management Assessment Grid, managers categorize employees as Stars, Worker Bees, Problem Employees, or Misplaced Employees. If you are a manager, the Management Assessment Grid can raise your awareness of how you may unconsciously categorize your staff. Some of these categorizations may be accurate; others may be unfair. Just by looking at the grid, you have probably already started thinking about different employees and where they fit. The explanations that follow will likely increase the strength of the associations you have begun to recognize. It is up to you to determine whether the categorizations you are making are fair, or if you need to reset your expectations to help your employees. If you are an employee, the Management Assessment Grid will help you understand how your manager formulates expectations of you and other team members. The tool will also increase your awareness of your own performance and potential. This simple recognition is the first step in helping you to move to higher levels of performance and service delivery or maintain those high levels if you are already there.

Star Employee

A Star is a top performer. The Star has valuable knowledge, skill, ability, and commitment to the institution and is respected by coworkers and managers. True Star employees are not only good at their jobs, but they also get along well with others. The Star brings both technical and relational competencies to the workplace.

Most Stars have worked a number of years in their fields to reach such high levels of success. For most of us, it takes a few years to develop, learn, and master our jobs and create professional networks and connections that are assets to our progression. Most Stars have gone through this process, so they do not require a lot of management oversight. Managers expect Stars to perform well.

If you are a Star employee, you can continue to be a Star as long as you meet two conditions. First, you must continually find new challenges. If you do not look for new learning opportunities within the scope of your job duties, you will become stagnant or bored. Opportunities are available through professional associations such as the National Association of Student Personnel Administrators, the American College Personnel Association, and many other national and regional associations that focus on specific functional areas within higher education. Second, Stars remain productive by mentoring others or working on committees or assignments that help the department or institution. Mentoring provides an opportunity for Stars to use their expertise to help others. Special assignments that combine operational activity with strategic contributions are most meaningful to Stars. Stars naturally become more interested in bigger-picture contributions as they advance in their careers, which is why the strategic contributions are particularly important. If you have mastered your job but are not involved in such professional associations, mentoring, or special projects, you will soon start to believe your job makes little difference—even though you are good at it.

Worker Bee Employee

The Worker Bee's primary assets are optimism and motivation. Much like the student who must work a bit harder to reach the goal, the Worker Bee must put in extra time to succeed. The extra effort pays dividends because performance is still high.

Higher education professionals who fit the Worker Bee profile are often new to the profession. New staff members typically need time to acculturate and learn the ropes. They need training even though they may come with the general knowledge that was a factor in their hiring. In some sense, there is no replacement for actual experience. Even for those professionals who have earned a master's degree in higher education administration, there is much to learn when starting out in a new position as a full-time employee.

A former Star may become a Worker Bee if there has been a major change in the department. New job assignments, changes in management or work procedures, or turnover within the team all require adjustment. The bigger the change, the more likely a Star will become a Worker Bee and have to learn and adapt.

If you are a Worker Bee, the solution to maintaining your performance is your attitude and perseverance. With the correct mentoring and training, which is usually dependent on your relationship with your manager, it is possible that you will become a Star if your talents are truly aligned with your job tasks. Without opportunities for improvement and learning, though, you risk burnout and frustration.

Problem Employee

Martin avoids the watercooler when Mark is there. Mark always has something or someone to complain about. If the foundation office has secured a major gift, Mark is the type of person who tells everyone that the gift should have been even bigger, or he is quick to point out the mistakes his colleagues made in settling for the final amount. It is also little surprise that Mark has well-known disagreements with his manager and coworkers. Mark is what is known as a Problem Employee.

Problem Employees do not perform to their potential. The cause of Problem Employees' difficulties is a certain level of discontent with other people or with themselves. Some Problem Employees are just chronic complainers who never see the positive side of others or their work. This employee's negative attitude overshadows any potential to become a Star. A Problem Employee's negative attitude also influences others.

Negative feelings and attitudes are often traced to interpersonal conflicts. Work environments are social environments, and conflicts and disagreements are inevitable. Thus, it is possible that a Problem Employee is a problem because he or she is unable to get along with another person. The person with whom the Problem Employee is having difficulty may be a manager or coworker. Terry worked as a tutor in academic support services at a large university. For two years, Terry worked alongside Michelle, who was in a similar position. Terry and Michelle did not get along during this entire time. By Terry's own admission, "it was a personality conflict" that was almost impossible to resolve. Terry was very good at her job, but she eventually decided to transfer to another department in the university. Her disagreements with Michelle were interfering with her work and affecting her performance. Terry is much happier in her new job in the graduate college. She still gets to work with students, and her performance evaluations are showing steady improvement.

A major source of disagreement or poor communication relates to change. Large changes may make Stars or Worker Bees feel as if they are starting all over again. It is the Stars and Worker Bees who are most successful in the current system, so they could perceive change as a threat to their success. Stars and Worker Bees are most likely to become Problem Employees if they truly believe the change is unnecessary, or they do not feel they were consulted before someone made the decision to change.

Another reason an employee with high potential may produce substandard results may simply be boredom or fatigue. The employee is in a rut. Problem Employees who fit this mold often have several years of successful experience but reach a burnout point. People who do not seek new learning opportunities to exercise their potential, either within the institution or through a professional association, quickly become Problem Employees.

Finally, Problem Employees may be experiencing personal problems that are affecting the work environment. Events in one part of life may influence events in another. Challenges or problems at home affect work. People experience child issues, divorce, health concerns, family deaths, or financial difficulties, and such problems can cause short-term lapses in performance.

Problem Employees need support. If they have a strong relationship with a coworker or manager, then it will be easy to find that support. An encouraging manager or colleague may help turn a Problem Employee into a Star. All of us work better in an environment where we have friends and people who are willing to support us through difficult times. Task-centered managers, in particular, may struggle with helping Problem Employees because, at the extreme, they believe home problems should not affect work performance. Another potential solution for a Problem Employee is a job change. Terry did not believe she could overcome her personality conflict with Michelle, so she found another job.

There are many reasons why a Problem Employee is a problem. If you find yourself exhibiting characteristics of a Problem Employee, the first step is to admit it and get at the root of the problem. Is it a problem with an internal customer? Are outside problems creeping into your work life? Do you have a disagreement with your manager? It is up to you to pinpoint the problem because managers (and everyone else in your office) very quickly and naturally form expectations about Problem Employees, and those expectations are difficult to alter if the problem lingers for too long.

Misplaced Employee

Misplaced Employees are those individuals who are experiencing serious problems or have not found a job that fits their talents. Misplacement can result because of poor relationships or lack of ability. Terry, from the academic support services example, was experiencing problems and, by her own admission, was a Problem Employee. If she had stayed in her position much longer, the situation would have deteriorated and she could have become a Misplaced Employee, not because of technical deficiency but interpersonal obstacles. The strained relationship between Michelle and Terry was escalating to such a point that the goals of the office were in jeopardy.

Misplaced Employees experience other challenges, many of which are similar to those of a Problem Employee: personal problems, change in job assignments, or miscommunication with management. Misplaced Employees who are experiencing temporary problems often need support, just as Problem Employees do. The challenge is that the depth of the problem is more serious and deep-rooted than is the case for a Problem Employee. If Terry had refused to leave academic support services, the problem also could have been solved if Michelle had left. But what if both refused to leave? In such a case, management intervention is inevitable, because, together, both Terry and Michelle become Misplaced Employees.

A common resolution for a Misplaced Employee is transfer or reassignment; in the worst-case scenario, it is termination. Retaining one or two Misplaced Employees could mean problems for an entire team. That is why it is important for the Misplaced Employee to recognize the misplacement or be told there is not a good fit. A person who is misplaced in one department may actually be a Star or Worker Bee in another. One hopes that a Misplaced Employee can look to managers or coworkers to help identify more appropriate career options. After all, a Misplaced Employee may be misplaced because of a flawed hiring decision.

Assessing Your Performance and Potential

The utility of the Management Assessment Grid is as much for employees as it is for managers. It is a self-awareness tool to assess your own performance and potential realistically. Your self-assessment of your own potential and performance is arguably the most important exercise you can complete. Where do you fall on the Management Assessment Grid? What category do you fit in, of the four shown in the grid? The eight questions in Exercise 15 will help you answer this.

The self-test in Exercise 15 gauges how you would describe yourself according to the Management Assessment Grid. Two additional questions may be useful to increase your self-awareness: (a) How would my manager classify me according to the Management Assessment Grid?, and (b) Is there a difference between how I classify myself and how my manager classifies me? Perhaps your manager would rate you as a Star because he or she makes several assumptions about what you can do, while your own rating falls under the Worker Bee category and you would actually prefer a little direction. You may have found that you describe yourself more generously than your manager does. This may be a signal to have a discussion with your manager to begin aligning expectations and perceptions about performance and service delivery.

EXERCISE 15 Self-Test for the Management Assessment Grid					
Answer the following questions based upon your first reaction, placing only one checkmark for each question under the number that best describes your response. Use the following scale: 1 = Strongly Disagree 2 = Disagree 3 = Neutral 4 = Agree 5 = Strongly Agree					
	1	**2**	**3**	**4**	**5**
1. I am successful at my job.					
2. Others view me as competent.					
3. I have a high level of knowledge and skill in regard to my job.					
4. My job evaluations are strong.					
5. My abilities fit well with my responsibilities.					
6. My manager is effective.					
7. I have strong, positive relationships with people on my team.					
8. Outside issues unrelated to my job have not affected my performance in a significant way.					

Instructions for Scoring:
- Add up your total score for the assessment by adding all individual item scores.
- Your score should be between 8 and 40.
- If you score is between 32 and 40, your classification is "Star."
- If your score is between 24 and 31, your classification is "Worker Bee."
- If your score is between 16 and 23, your classification is "Problem Employee."
- If your score is 15 or lower, your classification is "Misplaced."

Every person is capable of moving from one category on the Management Assessment Grid to another, but it starts with self-assessment and self-awareness. The self-test is a tool that tells you about your performance today and possibly raises questions about your potential for the future. Tools can help you match your knowledge, skill, and ability to your current job or another one on your campus. It is through this process that you will reach your potential, produce top-level service to internal and external customers, and create positive relationships with your manager and colleagues.

Managerial Influence Summary

The employee-manager relationship is the foundation that defines service delivery in any higher education office. Managers and employees should have an explicit understanding of different management styles and how those styles influence the employee-manager relationship and, ultimately, service delivery. The Management Assessment Grid is a tool to help both groups understand how perceptions and realities about performance and potential further influence the employee-manager dynamic. Employees who find themselves in the Problem or Misplaced categories of the Management Assessment Grid can take action to improve their performance, but the first step is assessment and acceptance. Star and Worker Bee employees must also take action and not assume that peak performance is guaranteed.

Chapter 7 Takeaways

- Both task-oriented and people-oriented managers have strengths and weaknesses. No one style is better than another in every situation and for managing every employee.
- Employees who understand and appreciate different management styles can work more effectively with their managers—in effect, they are better able to manage their managers.
- The low performance of Problem or Misplaced Employees may be attributed to attitudinal, technical, or relational issues, but an honest assessment of the issue is the first step toward solving the problem.
- Star and Worker Bee Employees must seek learning opportunities and work challenges to maintain high performance.

ACHIEVING SERVICE
EXCELLENCE

T he higher education industry has a rich and powerful tradition. The twin goals of providing academic and social growth for all students remain worthy ones for community colleges and universities and are embraced by virtually every faculty and staff member working in higher education. Some concepts associated with the business world, like customer service, have made their way into institutions and raised considerable controversy. The reality is that customer service has always been a part of higher education, but it is the misperceptions associated with it that raise concerns. In the end, higher education professionals who embrace the values and ideals associated with true customer service do not have to feel like they are compromising the traditions of the academy. Excellent service delivery is an institutional asset that can add to and even strengthen the traditions we value.

So how can your institution achieve service excellence? In this book, we illustrate that internal and external service excellence is predicated on many factors: defining service, understanding customers, managing for service excellence, and working to build a service culture. Customer service delivery is simultaneously a team and individual effort. Many of the exercises and assessments throughout this book can generate powerful insights when team members complete them individually but then discuss them collectively. Comparing lists that describe good and bad customer service, for example, creates productive discussion and, ultimately, some degree of convergence about the type of service team members believe their department should deliver.

Even if customer service has become a part of your institution's DNA, it is still important to personalize the general service question that we asked about your institution: How can your institution achieve service excellence? The question then becomes how can you, as a higher education professional, achieve excellent service delivery? Chapters 1–7 provide the tools to help you achieve service excellence; they lay the groundwork for implementation. Whether implementation actually happens depends on three things: commitment, attitude, and action.

Service Excellence = Commitment + Attitude + Action

Commitment, attitude, and action are the three ingredients that determine whether you are personally implementing and sustaining excellent service delivery. Let's examine each ingredient as it applies to you. If you are working through this book with your team, discuss your personal reflections after you have read each section. A team discussion will help you gauge your department, division, or institution's collective ability to achieve sustainable and excellent service delivery.

Commitment

People who are committed to service excellence know why their jobs are important. They know their work has meaning, and they believe they are providing something valuable to the customer. If you feel like you are providing a service that delivers value, your motivation and effort to produce excellence flows naturally.

True commitment is only possible if your professional values and beliefs match those of your organization. People change jobs or even careers because their values and beliefs are not aligned with the organization's service culture. Jim had such an experience. He was always good with numbers, earned an MBA, and, like most people in his cohort, went to work for a large multinational company. Jim's product portfolio for which he had fiscal responsibility included several tobacco products. Jim worked hard and produced sound financial analyses that helped improve efficiencies and increase profits. Jim's managers appreciated the quality of his work, but they sensed he hadn't totally bought into the company. As a result, every time there was a supervisory opening, Jim was overlooked. After three years of long hours and roadblocks to advancement, Jim reevaluated his situation and decided that he wanted to use his analytical skills to contribute to education. Both of his parents worked in higher education, so Jim was able to tap some networks and gain entrée into an institutional research office at a large multicampus community college system on the East Coast.

Jim never felt like he fit in with the multinational company's culture. Even though he did not pass judgment on those who were excited about the company's products and strategies, Jim was not. He did not believe in the products he was supporting. Jim's work was solid, but his managers correctly sensed his lack of commitment. Jim is making somewhat less as an institutional researcher than he was as a financial analyst, but today he is using his talents to produce analyses that he finds meaningful. Jim grew up around educators, and he believes in the value of education. He has been in meetings where his work informs high-level decisions about college access, equity, and affordability, all topics he is passionate about. As a professional working in institutional research, Jim feels committed to his job and to the multicampus system.

We all find value in different things, so what is important to one person may not be to another. If you believe the service you provide is important, whatever it is, you will feel your job makes a difference. This feeling translates into commitment. A heartfelt commitment means that you will do your job with enthusiasm and deliver excellent customer service because you believe in what you do. Without commitment, there is no emotional connection. Like Jim, you may go through the motions and produce good work, but until you feel commitment, you will never be truly motivated. People who are not committed cannot sustain high levels of service delivery.

Exercise 16 asks four questions to help you think about the meaning you attach to your job as it relates to the service you deliver. The questions will help you think about your commitment to your institution, department, and internal and external customers. You may find that these questions validate the importance and value of what you do. Conversely, the questions may lead you in another direction and encourage you to initiate a discussion with your manager or a colleague. At the extreme, your answers may indicate that you need to assess whether new responsibilities or maybe even a new position may reignite your professional commitment.

The questions start at the institutional level because it is helpful for each of us to reflect on the mission and purpose of our organizations and consider our service delivery within that context. You may work at an institution that seeks to maximize access, for example, and discover that your role in student services provides a necessary support that actually enables students to maintain their enrollment beyond initial entry. If you work in student affairs, you may find that your department contributes to the institution's goal of social development for its students.

The questions can help you connect your activity to the broader purpose of your functional area and institution. If you find the connection meaningful, you probably feel a strong commitment to your job and your institution. If you do not find the connection meaningful, then you probably do not feel as committed.

People who work through the questions in Exercise 16 commonly reflect on their institution's vision, mission, and values. They think about words like *integrity*, *responsibility*, *excellence*, and *passion* but may feel that these values are not practiced every day in the institution, or by certain people. If you had a similar experience, remember that mission, values, and goals are the ideals that everyone works to achieve. That does not mean that every interaction and every situation will exemplify these ideal values. People, including presidents, provosts, directors, supervisors, and colleagues, make mistakes. Sometimes we react to a difficult customer inappropriately. The mission, values, and goals remain important, though, because they help connect us to the things we should be thinking about, the things we should strive for. If you believe in the ideals of your institution and, in general, that your colleagues and administrators are working toward those ideals, then you shouldn't let periodic mistakes or lapses derail your commitment.

EXERCISE 16
Commitment: Connecting Purpose and Contribution

1. What is the purpose of your institution?

2. How does your department or division contribute to this purpose?

3. What are the main services you produce and deliver?

4. How does your work contribute to the department, division, or institution?

Many factors influence your commitment to internal and external customer service delivery, ranging from how you feel about your institution and colleagues to your actual job duties. Exercise 16 offers four guiding questions to help you think about your commitment to service delivery. It is important to think about how deeply committed you feel because commitment is a critical ingredient in the excellent service equation.

Service Attitude

When you believe in what you do, it isn't very hard to motivate yourself to work on your tasks. A strong commitment fuels a strong service attitude. But attitude is also influenced by emotions of the moment, and these fluctuate. It takes conscious effort to overcome fleeting emotions and sustain a positive attitude that matches one's deeper commitment. If effort can influence attitude and overcome the emotional lows we all experience, then it follows that attitude is a choice.

The psychology of the mind is a critical factor in determining not only attitude but also individual happiness and overall health. What Dr. Martin Seligman and other pioneers in positive psychology have found is that positive, conscious choices lead to happy and healthy lives. Norman Cousins became famous after he decided the antidote for a debilitating illness was six months of laughter therapy. Cousins repeatedly watched funny movies and television shows over a six-month period. To doctors' amazement, Cousins's disease had somehow disappeared. Apparently his positive attitude had stimulated body-curing endorphins, which played a central role in his recovery.

If we choose to focus on the positive, we will have a powerful service attitude to match our service commitment. Like Norman Cousins, we must make the choice to adopt a positive attitude. We may not cure diseases, but we will solve customer service problems and help build a progressive service culture in our institutions.

A positive attitude is difficult to maintain in the face of uncontrollable events and uncertainty. Community colleges and universities have combined, merged, and eliminated departments, positions, and services over the last several years as they search for efficiencies and deal with funding declines. Online providers and policymakers have increasingly focused the public's attention on the economic costs and benefits of higher education. This focus generates uncertainty for professionals who work in departments and divisions that contribute to the social and cultural development of students and society. The changing dynamics surrounding higher education means that there are many unknowns. Through all of this, the key to a positive attitude remains: Focus on those things that you can control. Author Jeffrey Gitomer, in the *Little Red Book of Selling*, advises us to resign our position as general manager of the universe. We should not worry about things we cannot affect. Instead, Gitomer counsels us to focus on those things we can influence, like our attitude and effort at work, or the way we treat internal and external customers.

There are times when you simply do not feel upbeat and motivated, so it is impossible to maintain a positive attitude constantly. We all have challenges and worries that generate internal anxiety. Paul Ekman, the famous professor from the University of California, San Francisco, who studies facial expressions and who wrote *Emotions Revealed*, offers some hope. He says that even on those days when things are not going well, you do not have to be overcome by what you are feeling on the inside. If you are suffering from a bad attitude, change from the outside in. Most of us believe that our facial expressions and body posture are reflections of how we feel on the inside. When we are sad or upset, our shoulders slump and our mouths turn downward. Ekman suggests that changing your facial expression from a frown to a smile actually changes your body chemistry on the inside and, thus, helps to change your attitude. He provides hope despite the challenges. Attitude is determined in your own mind and influenced by how you carry yourself.

The following ten points are not unique or the exclusive wisdom of any one person. They represent a collection from colleagues, customers, friends, and readings. They are simple and will help you develop or maintain a positive attitude, complement your commitment, and contribute to lasting service delivery:

Ten Positive Service Attitude Reminders
    1. Smile at people and make eye contact.
    2. Make humor a part of your life.

3. Whether on the phone or talking face-to-face, make sure your voice, body posture, and facial expressions all reflect a positive attitude.
4. Thank people for small things.
5. Call people by name.
6. Remember that your service to others is a reward in itself.
7. Make an effort to listen to or read positive material.
8. If you have to resolve a disagreement with a colleague, be the one to initiate a discussion.
9. At the start of every day, choose a positive attitude.
10. Connect daily tasks to your larger purpose.

Service Action

Service Question: What do you call a person who is committed to a cause and has a great attitude but never gets around to taking the action to make things happen?

a. Unemployed
b. A philosopher
c. A procrastinator
d. All of the above

The answer to the question is: d. All of the above. We have all met people who fervently believe in their institution. They can state the goals of their department, and they exhibit an infectious positive mental attitude. There is only one problem. Vision and passion go nowhere without steps that guide the passion and move toward the vision to which they are so committed. There is no action. These are the people who are philosophers (or office sages) because they have all the answers and can tell us what to do even though they have not shown that they can do it themselves. These are the people with big plans—but they never get moving on those plans.

Action is associated with activity, with doing. There are many paths to action, and the intent of *Creating a Service Culture in Higher Education Administration* is to provide application tools, assessments, and exercises that move you to action. If you have completed the assessments and exercises, then you have already taken the first step to deliver excellent customer service and contribute to a culture that can sustain it. The tools and exercises also serve as commonsense reminders to keep on doing the things you should be doing and avoid doing the things you know you should not be doing. An additional path toward action is to discuss the various assessments and exercises with your team. Team discussion generates insights that do not surface through our individual efforts.

If you have read this book, you may be eager for action just because you work in higher education. Those of us who have dedicated our careers to higher education find commitment to be the easy part of the Service Excellence equation at the beginning of the chapter. We are passionate about the role our institutions play in the lives of our students and how they enrich our communities. We believe in the value of a college degree, for both the economic and social opportunities it presents. We understand how our roles as managers, faculty, and staff fit into this larger purpose. The key, then, to achieving sustainable service excellence is to take action. You will notice that the actions that emanate from the assessments and exercises throughout this book are small steps. But these small steps lead to big results. Notice how internal customers respond to someone who is always willing to help, without complaint or expectation of reward. Notice how a positive attitude and a focus on service make your external customers feel. Notice how internal and external customers respond when you ask them if you have helped them, how you can help them, or if you can do more for them. These are all small action steps that make a very big difference in creating a service culture in higher education.

For any institution, true service delivery is achieved only through committed and motivated people—the professionals who make the institution what it is. Believe in the ideals of higher education and your institution and do everything within your power to become a servant of others. Find joy in service. You just may be the person responsible for starting a true customer service culture in your institution.